Twelve

Twelve Truths to Find Rest for Your Weary Soul

Written by Amber Peterson

Twelve: Twelve Truths to Find Rest for Your Weary Soul

Copyright © 2025 Amber Peterson

ISBN: 9798315653073

All rights reserved. No part of this publication may be reproduced, distributed, or transmitted in any form or by any means, including photocopying, recording, or other electronic or mechanical methods, without the prior written permission of the publisher, except in the case of brief quotations embodied in critical reviews and certain other noncommercial uses permitted by copyright law.

First Printing: 2025
Creator of Media Elements Used on Book Cover: ©Mila Kotova via Canva.com

All Scripture quotations, unless otherwise indicated, are taken from the Holy Bible, New International Version®, NIV®. Copyright ©1973, 1978, 1984, 2011 by Biblica, Inc.™ Used by permission of Zondervan. All rights reserved worldwide. www.zondervan.comThe "NIV" and "New International Version" are trademarks registered in the United States Patent and Trademark Office by Biblica, Inc.™

This book is written as a source of information only. The information contained in this book should not be considered a substitute for the advice, decisions, or judgment of the reader's physician or other professional advisor.

Some personal names and identifying details have been changed to protect the privacy of the individuals involved.

Any internet addresses, phone numbers, or company or product information printed in this book are offered as a resource. They are not intended in any way to be or to imply an endorsement by the author, nor does the author vouch for the existence, content, or services of these sites, phone numbers, companies, or products beyond the life of this book.

Dedication

This book, and every moment that brought its words to life, are dedicated to my gracious and loving God.

Thank you for seeing me, hearing me, and loving me always. Thank you for taking me on this twelve-day journey to be reminded of who You are and to see You more clearly than I ever had before. Thank you for providing me with the strength, faith, courage, and trust that I needed to put these words on paper and to be willing to share them with others. I surrender this book entirely to You. May the contents of this book continue to be used for Your glory and my good.

Dear Reader

Music plays a prominent role in this book, just as it does in my life. I have created a Spotify playlist that includes the songs mentioned in the book, which you can listen to as you read along. Scan the QR code below to be directed to the playlist. I pray these songs are a tremendous blessing to you as they have been to me.

Contents

Introduction 9

Chapter 1: "You Can Rest" 17

Chapter 2: "Though You Slay Me" 31

Chapter 3: "Goodness of God" 45

Chapter 4: "Firm Foundation" 59

Chapter 5: "I'm Listening" 71

Chapter 6: "Brokenness Aside" 87

Chapter 7: "Perfectly Loved" 101

Chapter 8: "Just as Good" 115

Chapter 9: "Highlands" 129

Chapter 10: "Evermore" 145

Chapter 11: "Falling in Love" 159

Chapter 12: "I Will Carry You" 175

Introduction

God sees you. God hears you. God loves you.

Here is what I know to be true of God's love.

God is *loving*. First John 4:9 says, "This is how God showed his love among us: He sent his one and only Son into the world that we might live through him."

God's love is *incomprehensible*. Ephesians 3:17-19 says:

> And I pray that you, being rooted and established in love, may have power, together with all the Lord's holy people, to grasp how wide and long and high and deep is the love of Christ, and to know this love that surpasses knowledge—that you may be filled to the measure of all the fullness of God.

God's love *fulfills*. Lamentations 3:22-23 says, "Because of the Lord's great love we are not consumed, for his compassions never fail. They are new every morning; great is your faithfulness."

God's love is *unfailing*. Psalm 36:5-7 says:

> Your love, Lord, reaches to the heavens, your faithfulness to the skies. Your righteousness is like the highest mountains, your justice like the great deep. You, Lord, preserve both people and animals. How priceless is your unfailing love, O God! People take refuge in the shadow of your wings.

TWELVE

God's love is *selfless*. Romans 5:8 says, "But God demonstrates his own love for us in this: While we were still sinners, Christ died for us."

God's love is a *gift*. Ephesians 2:4-5 says, "But because of his great love for us, God, who is rich in mercy, made us alive with Christ even when we were dead in transgressions—it is by grace you have been saved."

I have known all of these things to be true for many years. However, not so long ago, I found myself wrestling with whether I would truly walk in that belief or just accept it as truth when life was comfortable and it was convenient to trust God.

After a long season of crying out to the Lord from a place of complete desperation, I started to wonder why, if I was longing for something that seemed to be in line with His Word and His will, He was not answering it in what I thought was a timely manner. There were things I had been waiting on for so long that I knew were desires He had given me. It was very clear from the beginning that these desires came from the Lord because they were things that were far beyond my natural comfort zone and abilities.

Those desires were: 1) to move to Vancouver, Canada, to a city that had captivated my heart back in 2015 while there on a vacation to partner with a church planter to serve alongside them in spreading the gospel, and 2) to adopt a precious son from a country with limited access to the gospel to be able to provide him a home, a family, unconditional love, and to share the hope of Christ with him.

And yet, there I sat. Waiting. It had been seven years of persistent prayer and pursuit of moving to Vancouver, and five years of persistent prayer and pursuit of adoption. We told our then-five-year-old son that

INTRODUCTION

someday "brother in Africa" would come home. We started the adoption process when he was just two months old.

If God was loving, which I knew He was, and wanted good things for His children, which I knew He did, and wanted His name to be proclaimed to the ends of the earth, which I knew He did, then why were these things so slow to come to fruition? The tension of all those things being true simultaneously had me mentally tied up for quite some time.

Many friends had said multiple times over those years:

- "I admire your ability to trust God."
- "You have such incredible faith to be able to wait as long as you have."
- "You are so patient."

Those words always left me feeling quite confused, as I knew the reality was that I did not have a choice. The fact was that I did not want to wait any longer. I was hurting deeply in the waiting while also daily reminding myself to trust it all into the Lord's hands. If I could have sped up the process with either one of those desires, I would have, but I had zero control over both situations.

While I certainly spent countless hours praying prayers of trusting the Lord, His timing, and His sovereignty over it all, truth be told, there were also many prayers filled with tears and confusion and crying out the words of the father of the sick son in Mark 9:24, "I do believe; help me overcome my unbelief!"

Absolutely nothing went according to plan or the estimated timelines I expected. It was almost always twice as long as expected, if not more. I'm a Westerner. I'm American. I'm type A. To put it another way, I

TWELVE

hold tightly to schedules and plans. The Lord was refining and growing me in surrendering that to Him in that particular season because it never went according to schedule.

In January 2022, I was walking the streets of Vancouver, Canada, alongside a group of students and adult sponsors for our third trip to spread the gospel alongside a local church to a city that had captivated my heart, when all of a sudden, it hit me. God had answered the *exact* prayer I had been praying for seven years. It looked nothing like I expected. It looked nothing like what I had specifically been praying for it to be. And yet, I could see that it was even more beautiful because I had served with nearly sixty people by that point in the very place the Lord had instilled a love for in my life so many years earlier.

How had I missed that?

How had I missed God's faithfulness? He had been fulfilling the deepest desires of my heart all along, but because it was not exactly as I expected it to be, I had overlooked it for years at that point. But God, in His grace and mercy, had patiently waited for me to open my eyes to see Him and His provision. He had been faithful through every single bit of it. He is always faithful. Remember Psalm 36:5-7 says:

> Your love, Lord, reaches to the heavens, your faithfulness to the skies. Your righteousness is like the highest mountains, your justice like the great deep. You, Lord, preserve both people and animals. How priceless is your unfailing love, O God! People take refuge in the shadow of your wings.

The rest of that week, the Lord used numerous people to overwhelm me with the realization that God sees me, God hears me, and

INTRODUCTION

God loves me. I left that trip somehow in the most broken and vulnerable place I had ever been, and yet also the most assured and confident of my belief in God that I had ever been. I did not realize that such opposing emotions and feelings could coexist in harmony. Even amid the brokenness, there was a presence of both grief and joy where the Lord was evident in each.

God sees me. God hears me. God loves me.

Those truths would be what I clung to for life and breath over the months that followed. Those months would consist of my life being turned upside down in every possible way. The Lord brought things out of the dark and into the light, which resulted in complete and total heartbreak. The little boy we had finally been matched with and were diligently working to bring home, we were no longer able to adopt. Our marriage also came crashing down right along with it, resulting ultimately in divorce. A pastor and his wife sat across from me at a local coffee shop as we talked through what had transpired in a very short amount of time. He said, "Amber, you have hit rock bottom. But there's only one way to go from rock bottom: up." We all knew that "up" was only possible through a complete and total surrender of it all to the Lord.

I remember telling them, through all the tears and the pain, that, though my heart could not have been more shattered than it was in that very moment, I had never seen God more clearly. That was the truth. God had made it abundantly clear to me that He sees me. He hears me. He loves me. Because of that, I knew one day God would restore me. One day, God would see me through to the other side of the valley of the shadow of death. He was not going to leave me in it.

TWELVE

That's where this story picks up.

The following eight months, I existed in a state of complete restlessness. I had walked through about eight months of very intense spiritual warfare at night in 2021 and 2022. I spent my nights with overwhelming and debilitating nightmares that had left me in a place of being scared to close my eyes at night. So, I just did not. I slept as little as possible. However, battling ongoing lies and spiraling thoughts was expending every ounce of mental energy I could muster throughout the night. You can only survive like that for so long.

By the fall, when I was able to slow down, my body came crashing down right along with it. I was struggling with ongoing headaches, joint pain, inflammation, exhaustion, and a body that was physically depleting with the amount of weight I was losing as a result of it all. I knew I needed rest more than anything, and I do not just mean sleep. I mean *real* rest that is found only in the Lord. Matthew 11:28 says, "Come to me, all you who are weary and burdened, and I will give you rest."

I have the joy of spending my days primarily in a Christian school, talking about Jesus with students. One day in December of 2022, I was proctoring a final at school. I was in a silent room for an extended period, gazing out at the students and periodically looking down to read Scripture. I had deleted all my social media accounts about six months before this point. I had seen early on how social media was quickly becoming both a coping mechanism to escape my own life and a source of extensive comparison, stirring up discontentment and jealousy. I knew I needed to fuel my thoughts and fill my mind with the truths of God's Word without distraction. My son needed my undivided attention in this particular

INTRODUCTION

season as he was also processing the separation and divorce of his parents, as well as the loss of a brother he had waited for right along with us. We both desperately needed Jesus to heal our hearts and restore our souls.

So, there I sat reading Psalm 91:1-2, "Whoever dwells in the shelter of the Most High will rest in the shadow of the Almighty. I will say of the Lord, 'He is my refuge and my fortress, my God, in whom I trust.'" I pondered those verses. I craved rest. I knew I needed rest more than anything else in that given moment, and I could only find rest in the ultimate refuge and fortress. So, I made a plan. I did something I had never done before. To be honest, my emotions were a mix of excitement and terror to do what I did.

I planned to take a trip with just me and Jesus. I am naturally a more independent person, but not quite to the point of adventuring on my own. But it was clear as day that I needed to take time to get away, press pause on the regular, daily hustle and bustle of life, and be with the Lord. I wanted to go somewhere where I could unplug and be in God's beautiful creation, just me and Him. I wanted to spend an extended amount of time praying, worshiping, reading, walking, and talking with Him.

I love the outdoors in general, but I have a particular fondness for the mountains. Being surrounded by the fingerprints of God as I look out in every direction is just unlike any other topography to me. As I prayed and thought about where I might go, I kept coming back to Wyoming and Montana. I planned a trip to Grand Teton, Glacier, and Yellowstone National Parks.

TWELVE

I spent twelve days being overwhelmed by God's incredible creation and His artistry in all of it. In a word, here's how I would describe each of the National Parks I visited: Grand Teton – idyllic, Glacier – ineffable, and Yellowstone – iconic.

Throughout the driving, exploring, reading, and simply being present with the Lord, I journaled extensively about the lessons He taught me along the way. Worship was also a significant component of the beauty of my time with the Lord on this trip. I mean, goodness, I was in my car for at least seventy hours driving by myself. Along with each lesson the Lord was showing and teaching me, there was a song He specifically used to speak to my heart at that particular time. I will be sharing each of those as I close out each chapter.

Twelve days.

Twelve songs.

Twelve glimpses into my heart.

Twelve truths of the unchanging character of God.

Since returning from that trip, I have continued to process everything God showed me during that time. That trip will forever hold a special place in my heart for a million reasons. I look forward to sharing just a few of those reasons with you.

I pray that, somehow, this outpouring of my heart reminds you that God sees you, God hears you, and God loves you.

Let's get to it! It all starts with Psalm 91:1-2.

Chapter 1

"You Can Rest"

Psalm 91:1-2 says, "Whoever dwells in the shelter of the Most High will rest in the shadow of the Almighty. I will say of the Lord, 'He is my refuge and my fortress, my God, in whom I trust.'"

While I was on that trip, the Lord constantly brought Psalm 91:1-2 to mind. There are a few key words that help establish the connection between these two verses. Psalm 91:1-2 says, "Whoever *dwells* in the shelter of the Most High will *rest* in the shadow of the Almighty. I will say of the Lord, 'He is my refuge and my fortress, my God, in whom I *trust*.'" According to this passage, simply put, as we *dwell* in God, we *trust* Him and receive *rest* as a result. The fruit is *rest*.

But what does that mean?

There is so much in Scripture about dwelling with God.

- Colossians 3:16 says, "Let the message of Christ dwell among you richly as you teach and admonish one another with all wisdom

TWELVE

through psalms, hymns, and songs from the Spirit, singing to God with gratitude in your hearts."

- Psalm 27:4 says, "One thing I ask from the Lord, this only do I seek: that I may dwell in the house of the Lord all the days of my life, to gaze on the beauty of the Lord and to seek him in his temple."
- Ephesians 3:16-17 says, "I pray that out of his glorious riches he may strengthen you with power through his Spirit in your inner being, so that Christ may dwell in your hearts through faith."

These are just a few examples of this word in Scripture, and yet we can already see this beautiful picture of an intimate relationship with God. He is our Creator. He is our Father. As our Creator and Father, He wants nothing more than for us to know Him. As we grow in our knowledge of Him, we form a deep relationship with Him. It is one of the many amazing gifts He blesses His children with, for which I am beyond thankful in my life.

As we truly pursue Him, we find that His character is unchanging throughout Scripture. We see again and again that He is someone we can trust wholeheartedly.

- Isaiah 26:4 says, "Trust in the Lord forever, for the Lord, the Lord himself, is the Rock eternal."
- Psalm 9:10 says, "Those who know your name trust in you, for you, Lord, have never forsaken those who seek you."
- Psalm 62:7-8 says, "My salvation and my honor depend on God; he is my mighty rock, my refuge. Trust in him at all times, you people; pour out your hearts to him, for God is our refuge."

"YOU CAN REST"

Maybe you are like me, and trust does not come quickly or easily. The beauty of Scripture is that we get to see Hebrews 13:8 on full display: "Jesus Christ is the same yesterday and today and forever." God's character has never changed. He is always faithful. As we begin to look for His heart on display throughout Scripture, we find that we can fully trust Him. Of course, that leads to rest. When you know that you are safe, secure, loved, cared for, and wrapped in compassion and grace, then naturally, rest would be what would follow.

I am a planner, like extremely organized, over-the-top, every 't' crossed and 'i' dotted kind of planner. I had researched every hike I planned to do on my trip. I had two primary goals for the time I was going to spend hiking: 1) to not get lost, and 2) to not get mauled by a bear. I have a fear of getting lost. I had not only researched the hikes but also downloaded maps for every trail, so I was not dependent on cell service to find my location. I had them all ready to go on my phone on my AllTrails app.

Everything had gone so smoothly in Grand Teton and Glacier National Parks up to this point. My last day in Glacier National Park was also my last day of hiking. The hike I was most looking forward to was finally going to take place on this very day.

I left the campground at 5:58 a.m. I drove across the Going-to-the-Sun Road from the far West side to the far East side. To get from Sprague Creek (West side) to Many Glacier (East side) took 1 hour and 45 minutes. I finally got there! I had been waiting for months to do the Grinnell Glacier hike. It was a ten-mile hike to a glacier! It was not an easy ten miles. In fact,

TWELVE

on AllTrails, it is classified as hard, but it has 4.9 stars with 6,500 reviews. I was determined to hike to the glacier.

In the summer, Glacier National Park requires vehicle reservations for entry. If you are camping in the park and have made a campsite reservation, then you do not need the vehicle reservation. That is what I did. However, when I arrived at Many Glacier, I was informed that the five-mile road to Many Glacier, including the trailhead for the Grinnell Glacier hike, required a separate pass. This pass needed to be reserved in advance, which I had not done. I will not lie, there were some small tears as a result of the disappointment in that moment. I was exhausted from waking up at 5:30 a.m., I had driven almost two hours, and all just to find out I had to turn around. But there I was.

On my drive the day before, I had heard the Drive Along tour mention the Highline Trail. The virtual tour guide said it was tough, but many people just hiked three miles in and then hiked back. I thought, "Well, if I was going to do ten hard miles, I can surely do six." With the limited service I had at that moment, I looked it up, and it had a 4.8-star rating with 2,300 reviews. I decided to do it.

Lesson #1: Read the details and the reviews, not just the stars.

This place was halfway between my campground and where I was at that moment. So, I turned around and drove back to that location, which was about an hour away. I got there at 9:00 a.m. and waited about forty-five minutes for parking. Unfortunately, this trail shares a parking lot with the most common trail in the park, the Hidden Lake Overlook. Finally, I parked and off I went.

"YOU CAN REST"

To get to this trailhead, you walk across the street, through a small area that is densely populated with trees, and then turn the corner. You cannot see the trailhead from the parking lot; that is how well the trees conceal it. I turned the corner and gasped out loud in complete and total fear. The trail *began* with a rope attached to a rock wall for a half-mile-long path. The path was narrow and had a *steep* drop-off. I literally laughed and thought, "What in the world have I gotten myself into?" I slowly took one step at a time and decided to press on.

I started walking and caught up to a family from Georgia who had their four and six-year-old boys with them. We walked and talked for about 1.5 miles. During that time, the dad asked me if I was going to do the whole hike. I told him I was just planning to do the three miles out and back. He then told me they were doing the entire thing, which they thought was twelve miles total, because coming back was more challenging than finishing the trail, according to what they had read. We were on a slow decline for a while, and he did say there would be a part that ascends some. The first eight miles would be smooth, but then the last four miles would be downhill. I decided to take him at his word and to do the whole hike.

Lesson #2: Never commit to a long hike if you do not know what you are getting yourself into.

Lesson #3: Never double your hiking distance without planning accordingly for your water and food supply.

Lesson #4: Never *ever* hike twelve miles in direct sunlight with only 40 oz of water.

TWELVE

I walked. At times, there was a break from the sun, accompanied by a delightful, much-appreciated gift of shade. But most of the hike was in direct sunlight. I started at around 10:00 a.m., and within just a few miles, it already started to feel quite warm. The high that day was around 90°F. Three miles in (my initial turnaround point), there was a massive pile of snow covering a large amount of space right by the trail. Now was the moment. I hesitated for a brief minute, but I decided just to do it. "How bad can it be?" I thought. That question is usually a sure sign you are going to regret your decision later.

I then met three girls from Florida. Right after the snow, there were several awful switchbacks; it was so hot, and the trail was in direct sunlight at that point. The four of us were attempting to make it up one step at a time. For a moment, I wondered if that was the worst of the incline that the Georgia family had informed me was going to take place. The answer to that would be no. No, it was not.

We were now about 6.5 miles into the twelve-mile hike, and I realized my water was gone. One mile from where we were was a chalet. We were sitting down eating because it was 1:00 p.m. by this time. The girls were eating their lunches, which they wisely packed. I was eating my snacks, which I thankfully put in my bag just in case I needed some for the six miles of hiking.

Right behind us was a spur off the trail to Grinnell Glacier, the very glacier I was planning to hike to that morning! It was only one mile away, two miles to go out and back. However, that mile was NO joke. We were listening to people come down and say verbatim that the way up is the absolute worst thing they have ever experienced, but the view is worth it!

"YOU CAN REST"

One guy told us he had completed several mountain top hikes, but that was the hardest thing he had ever done. However, he also said it was beautiful. The girls and I sat there for a while discussing whether we were going to do it, but none of us were brave enough to be the first one to say yes.

One of the girls decided to do it. I could either head to the chalet a mile away, where I knew there was water, or continue with the hike. It was only two miles. I decided to go for it.

Lesson #5: One mile of straight-up hiking in 90°F without any shade whatsoever, as well as without water, is *never* a good idea.

One girl who had come down told us that she counted her steps, and every time she reached thirty, she sat down and took a breath before continuing, because the incline was that intense. That is what I did, especially since I had no water.

These three girls from Florida and I made our way up this massive side of a mountain. We finally made it to the top! The glacier was magnificent! The blue color of the glacier was so vibrant, especially against the backdrop of pure, white snow, the beautiful green mountains, and the perfect, clear blue sky on a sunny day surrounding it. It was such a picturesque moment!

Someone informed us that we had only made it 0.8 miles; there were 0.2 more miles to go to get the most incredible view of three lakes with the glacier. This girl from Florida and I looked at each other, took a huge deep breath, and decided we were going to do it.

Here's the deal. We followed this little trail over to a giant rock that marked the remaining .2 miles, when suddenly the very trail we were

TWELVE

standing on disappeared. The rock was so steep that we literally could not see the trail to get up. We thought there had to be one, but we could not find it anywhere. We truly got on our hands and knees and scrambled our way up the side of this mountain on loose rocks. I genuinely prayed as I reached for the next rock that I did not grab onto a loose rock and end up sliding down the entire mountainside.

By God's grace, we made it to the top. It was breathtaking! The 360° view was unreal. There was this awe-inspiring row of pristine lakes, the Grinnell Glacier, and mountain peaks on one side, but then you turned around, and in every direction, it was rolling hills and mountains as far as the eye could see. I will never forget that very moment.

Now that we were at the top, we could see the path to get down. We had a nice laugh at ourselves and the fact that we took the hardest humanly possible path up that .2 stretch, but we had no idea.

Lesson #6: Do not scramble up the side of a mountain on loose rocks when there is a path.

I then realized I was in a time crunch. The girls had parked at the end of the trail. I had parked at the trailhead. I had to catch a shuttle to get back to my car. The last shuttle was going to come around 6:30 p.m. It was about 4:00 p.m. at that point. I had one mile to return from this little excursion, one mile to fetch water at the chalet (Lord willing), and four miles of a 3,000-foot descent to reach the shuttle. One of the girls shared some of her extra water with me, which was life-saving. I drank the water as fast as possible, and then parted ways with them while they recovered from the climb.

"YOU CAN REST"

As fast as I possibly could, I descended the mile from the overlook and walked the mile to the chalet. No lie, I paid $18.25 for a water bottle and a Gatorade that were lukewarm, and it was the best water and Gatorade I have had in my whole life.

Lesson #7: Always pack far more water than you need, especially if you are someone who can easily double or triple your hiking distance without a second thought.

I then started the last four-mile descent. By this time, it was 4:45 p.m. I hoped I could make it. I had been told by several people that the last four miles were great because they were only downhill, but that they were also challenging due to the steepness. It was also in perfect bear terrain. I had been avoiding hiking alone in bear country after having a solo bear encounter at Jenny Lake. I started jogging for about a mile until I caught up with a precious couple from California. We were all walking quickly, but their car was also at the end of the trail. People who researched this trail knew something I did not.

Lesson #8: Again, read all the details about a hike before you embark on it.

While we walked, they asked why I was out there by myself. I told them I had recently walked through a few difficult years that had brought me to a place where I needed to unplug and be with the Lord in His creation. She then told me that a friend of hers, a psychology professor, had shared how healing nature can be in the more difficult seasons of life. I shared with her that while nature is therapeutic, I believe true healing can only take place from the One who created all the beauty that we observe through nature. Nature reflects His intentionality and creativity in such a

TWELVE

beautiful way. I was there to be with Him and enjoy His presence. I truly meant that.

We arrived at the bottom at 6:20 p.m. The shuttle was already there waiting for us. I ran to the shuttle and collapsed into the seat. I finished what little water I had remaining. When the shuttle dropped me off at the trailhead, I refilled my water and drank all 40 oz. of it.

A couple of hours later, I had made it back to my campsite. What I thought was going to be six miles, then thought it was going to be twelve miles, ended up being 14.9 miles! It was the most beautiful scenery I have ever seen on a hike, while also being physically the hardest thing I have ever done. But everyone was right, every part of it was worth it.

Now, here is the point of that story. There will be times when we find ourselves in a place where we feel uncertain about where to go. There are going to be moments or even seasons where you feel lost in the dark. There will be days when you cry out to God and ask Him to show you where to go or what to do because you cannot see even the tiniest hint of a path. But do you know who does? The Creator of all things sees exactly where you need to go and what you need to do.

He does not show us the entire path from the very beginning. There are probably a million reasons why that is, but one of them is that even if we wanted to, we would not be able to understand. Isaiah 55:8-9 says, "'For my thoughts are not your thoughts, neither are your ways my ways,' declares the Lord. 'As the heavens are higher than the earth, so are my ways higher than your ways and my thoughts than your thoughts.'"

So often, we just want to stand at the top of the mountain and know precisely where God is leading us. We want to see the result. We want to know if He is expecting us to go six, twelve, or fifteen miles. But instead, we are at the beginning of that hike, holding onto the rope against the wall, clinging tightly to the Lord, trusting that He is secure. He may not tell us how long we will be in that place, but He does show us the next right step.

But for Him to do that, we have to seek Him. To trust Him, we have to know Him. We have to dwell with Him. We have to spend time getting to know Him, not just His Word. The New Testament contains stories of people Jesus rebuked, who knew His Word forward and backward but did not know Him at all.

We want to know the heart of God. We want to know His character. He has revealed so much about Himself to us in Scripture, but it is so easy for us to study His Word and miss Him. That happened over and over in Scripture. I pray it would not happen to us.

We want to know Him. We want to dwell in Him. As our trust grows, we find ourselves no longer worrying about where He will have us in six, twelve, or fifteen years, but instead we rest in where He has us right now. We may be in the most challenging situation we could ever imagine, but trusting Him through it is worth it.

My question to you is, do you trust God?

Do you really trust Him?

I am not asking you something I have not had to ask myself many times in life. People in my life have hurt me whom I should have been able to trust. I have gone through really dark seasons where it felt like life was too overwhelming, and it would have been easy to think God was nowhere to be found. My sin has weighed so heavily on me at times that the weight

TWELVE

felt like it might just crush me. But those moments also showed me more than any other moments in my life that God truly leads us through the valley of the shadow of death (Psalm 23:4). He does not leave us in it. He never leaves us or forsakes us (Hebrews 13:5-6). God's light shines so brightly even in the darkest places if we will just open our eyes and look for Him.

We can trust Him.

Do you trust Him?

When He does not answer a prayer as quickly as you would like or with the answer you would like, do you trust that He knows what is best?

When it feels like your world is falling apart, do you trust Him to be able to carry you through that hard season?

When someone you should have been able to trust seriously lets you down, do you believe you can trust God?

When you are overwhelmed by guilt and shame because of the sin you are struggling with, do you trust Him to be gracious and forgiving when you turn to Him?

When you feel like God made a mistake in the way He has made you, do you trust that He sees you as perfectly and wonderfully made?

Do you trust Him?

If not, what is it about God you need to seek out in Scripture to understand more of? I promise you will find it. God's Word is a gift given to us to reveal His heart to us. From Genesis to Revelation, we see that He is intentional. He is loving. He is kind. He is patient. He is good.

"YOU CAN REST"

To find the rest we so desperately long for, we must trust in God. To trust in God, we have to know Him. To know Him, we have to dwell in His presence. Get to know Him. He will change your life.

In a season where I desperately needed rest, I found that the only way I was going to experience the rest I needed was to release control and rest in the One who has all control. This song constantly reminds me of that truth. Take a moment to pause and listen to the words of "You Can Rest" by Hillary Scott.

I pray wherever you find yourself today that you find hope in the truth of the unchanging character of God.

- *You may feel overcome by fear or feel completely alone, but you can rest in the One who is faithful to keep His promises.*

God sees you. God hears you. God loves you.

Chapter 2

"Though You Slay Me"

James 1:2-4 says, "Consider it pure joy, my brothers and sisters, whenever you face trials of many kinds, because you know that the testing of your faith produces perseverance. Let perseverance finish its work so that you may be mature and complete, not lacking anything."

A few years after graduating from college, I started attending a women's Bible study at my church. We studied the book of James as we walked through a study written by Beth Moore. Up to that point in my life, my Scripture memory had consisted of memorizing a verse, or at most, three consecutive verses scattered throughout Scripture. However, I vividly remember my reaction to the challenge Beth Moore gave to memorize the *entire* book of James to kick off the Bible study. I thought she was crazy! Who in their right mind can memorize an *entire* book of the Bible? That was unheard of to me.

TWELVE

And yet, I welcomed the challenge. I was intimidated, to say the least. And in a measure of complete and total honesty, I think I only made it through three of the five chapters during that Bible study. However, it brought Scripture to life in a profoundly radical way in my life. There was a fire that started in that season that I had never tapped into in my faith journey up to that point. I will forever be grateful to Beth Moore for how God used her in my life then and still to this day.

Scripture memory is a practice we desperately need in our lives, yet I often find myself struggling with the challenges of time and persistence in completing it. I know I am not alone in that struggle. Know that you are not alone in that struggle either.

To this day, James 1 has been a chapter of the Bible that I have returned to more times than I can count. Romans 8 might be the only chapter that beats it out for my constant reference back to the truths found in a particular chapter, but we will come back to that chapter later.

The entire book of James is a gut punch if we are being honest. He draws upon numerous passages from the Gospels throughout Jesus' ministry and ultimately paints a picture of what a follower of Christ should exemplify in their daily life. James 1:22 says, "Do not merely listen to the word, and so deceive yourselves. Do what it says." It is clear that James truly is dedicated to moving beyond just hearing and into action.

That sounds all fine and dandy until you realize James 1:22 follows James 1:2-4. He had just told the Jewish Christians at that time to respond to *trials* with *joy*. That should be an absolute contradiction. Why on earth would you ever rejoice when experiencing difficult circumstances in life?

I am glad you asked.

"THOUGH YOU SLAY ME"

While driving through Glacier and Yellowstone National Parks, there were parts of both parks that had experienced previous forest fires, the effects of which were still evident in the remains today. Our first response when seeing something like that is to view it as a total loss, destroyed, and nothing more than a wasteland. That was most certainly my first reaction when looking out over the remains of bare trees that fires had marred. What was once green and lush was now black and gray. What once had life was now lifeless, so it seemed.

Throughout my time, I would pass by these areas, and initially I just looked up at the standing remains of trees that had life sucked right out of them. They would never recover. They would never be able to produce fruit again. They were just ruins in what I saw as a desolate land.

The Guide Along tour had mentioned several times that unless a forest fire is going to cause damage to a structure of some kind, park rangers will let it burn because some of the trees and plants in the forests grow back even stronger after a fire by design. The trees and plants anticipate a fire. Some plants get choked out by the shadows of the trees, and they quickly resurface after a fire passes through. It can also become too difficult for animals to navigate the forests if the trees continue to grow and spread without ever stopping.

One day, while looking out over the remains of a forest fire, my perspective changed. It finally resonated with me about the third or fourth time I heard the Guide Along tour give the same spiel about these forest fires (sometimes I can be a slow learner). For some reason, this time I truly heard what he was saying.

TWELVE

He began talking about the lodgepole pines that are abundant throughout Yellowstone National Park. These trees are incredibly tall and dense in the forests. Remarkably, these trees are capable of surviving after a forest fire.

You see, cones protect the seeds that are necessary for lodgepole pines to reproduce. That is no different than many other evergreen trees, right? But wait, there is more. A special resin seals these cones. This resin requires an incredibly high degree of heat to melt away, allowing the seeds to be released. The only way for these seeds to be released, allowing the trees to continue reproducing, is for a fire to pass through the area. It is almost as if God planned for these trees to depend upon forest fires! Oh, wait, He did!

After hearing this multiple times, I finally started looking down at the ground rather than up at the barren remains of the trees. I was able to see the new growth, the plants and trees that had begun to resurface. There were tall pine trees burned to a crisp, while the ground was covered with lush green bushes, berries, wild flowers, and trees slowly regrowing. It was beautiful to see the restoration naturally taking place in this area, which one might think would remain dead.

Then it hit me like a ton of bricks! This new life, even amid tragedy, is a real-life example of James 1:2-4! These trees require harsh conditions to mature fully. They cannot reproduce without it. This realization was a full-on Miley Cyrus "Wrecking Ball" moment for me. (And yes, I just went there.) The difficult moments in our lives refine us just as much as they do the trees and plants in a forest after a fire. Christ has given us a gift to see us through the fire.

"THOUGH YOU SLAY ME"

First Corinthians 10:13 says, "No temptation has overtaken you except what is common to mankind. And God is faithful; he will not let you be tempted beyond what you can bear. But when you are tempted, he will also provide a way out so that you can endure it." There is a linchpin to this passage, though. Do not miss it. He is not saying that He will never allow us to endure things that are too much for us on our own. I can think of many things that are beyond our ability to walk through on our own. I have endured many of them throughout my life. He finishes that verse by saying He will provide a way out so that we can endure it. Scripture portrays God as our strength.

- Habakkuk 3:19 says, "The Sovereign Lord is my strength; he makes my feet like the feet of a deer, he enables me to tread on the heights."
- Isaiah 40:29-31 says, "He gives strength to the weary and increases the power of the weak. Even youths grow tired and weary, and young men stumble and fall; but those who hope in the Lord will renew their strength. They will soar on wings like eagles; they will run and not grow weary, they will walk and not faint."
- Psalm 28:7-8 says, "The Lord is my strength and my shield; my heart trusts in him, and he helps me. My heart leaps for joy, and with my song I praise him. The Lord is the strength of his people, a fortress of salvation for his anointed one."

Moments that seem like they may ultimately defeat us do not stand a chance because the Lord provides the strength. He gives us the ability to endure. Initially, it may look like destruction has overtaken everything, but the Lord brings new growth. He is not surprised by the

TWELVE

consuming situations that catch us off guard and overwhelm us like a wildfire. He knew it was coming all along. And the beautiful thing is, He will restore life through it. He even allows hidden away parts of us to grow, thrive, and shine that the darkness may have choked out before.

Isaiah 61:2-3 says:

He has sent me to bind up the brokenhearted, to proclaim freedom for the captives and release from darkness for the prisoners, to proclaim the year of the Lord's favor and the day of vengeance of our God, to comfort all who mourn, and provide for those who grieve in Zion— to bestow on them a crown of beauty instead of ashes, the oil of joy instead of mourning, and a garment of praise instead of a spirit of despair. They will be called oaks of righteousness, a planting of the Lord for the display of his splendor.

The beauty of the Lord is that difficult experiences only make us stronger. Why? These challenging moments we have can lead to an undeniable and unwavering hope. We begin to reproduce our faith (also known as discipleship) after seeing God's incredible ability to restore our lives, regardless of the hardships we have faced, because He takes the broken parts of our lives and makes them whole. You cannot *not* talk about the transforming work of the gospel when you have experienced it personally.

In Mark 1:40-45, we see such a fascinating miracle. A man with leprosy is crying out to Jesus for healing. We are not told many details about his life. We have no idea how long he was isolated from his family and his community outside of the main city due to his leprosy. We do not know how severe his leprosy was or how much it had overtaken his body. Although we may not know the length of time, we can tell he had reached a point of total despair. In his distress and anguish, he cries out to Jesus to heal him.

Jesus heals him and makes the most interesting request of him. In Mark 1:44, Jesus says, "See that you don't tell this to anyone. But go, show yourself to the priest and offer the sacrifices that Moses commanded for your cleansing, as a testimony to them." Jesus did not just heal this man physically of an ailment that had become bothersome; He also healed him spiritually. By healing his physical body, Jesus restored life to him! He was able to be a part of his family again. He was able to work again. He was able to worship again. Jesus completely transformed him!

Now, what I find particularly interesting is that Jesus expected him to say nothing. There has been speculation about why this is the case. Still, the bottom line that we see in passages that follow this particular event is a constant reiteration from Jesus that physical healing is only part of the story. To those He encounters, He emphasizes again and again the need for spiritual healing. Salvation is what ultimately matters because it changes our eternity.

We all have an eternity at stake. At the right time, Jesus began to proclaim this message of salvation that would only be available through Him. To this day, we can still experience the forgiveness of our sins through the life, death, burial, and resurrection of Jesus. He made a way, the only way, to restore our relationship with God.

For whatever reason, Jesus was not yet ready to share that message at that point. He knew when the time would come that hearts

TWELVE

would be prepared to hear that message, but it was not quite yet. But of course, the man runs and tells everyone exactly what Jesus did. If we are being honest, I would have done the same thing. It is tough to keep something to yourself that is the best thing that has ever happened to you!

So, then, why are we so afraid to share the transforming work of Christ in our own lives? We know that it comes through a recognition of the sin we have committed. We often quote Romans 3:23, "For all have sinned and fall short of the glory of God," and then live as if it only applies to everyone else. We often convince ourselves that no one could handle knowing that we are not perfect.

We also find ourselves often turning to Romans 6:23, "For the wages of sin is death, but the gift of God is eternal life in Christ Jesus our Lord." But do we *really* believe that we deserve death? Do we *really* believe that we deserve hell, eternal separation from a holy God?

Without the gift of grace and mercy found in the shedding of Christ's blood, we would have no hope (Hebrews 9:22). Yet we are scared to admit that we have things in our lives that God needs to prune, destroy, eradicate, or whatever other means He may need to use to rebuild us and make us even stronger. But, goodness, there is so much beauty in standing with Paul in the truth of Galatians 2:20, "I have been crucified with Christ and I no longer live, but Christ lives in me. The life I now live in the body, I live by faith in the Son of God, who loved me and gave himself for me." That is worth screaming from the rooftops!

One night of my trip, I was sitting at my picnic table eating dinner. I realized that lodgepole pines were surrounding my campsite. I looked up and saw a little peephole of a clear blue sky creeping through the trees all around me, which were teaching me more than I could contain in that moment. I just started weeping.

I found myself releasing this reality to the Lord, that life had not gone according to plan up to that moment. Just about everything had gone against every plan I had ever made. And yet, I was still standing. I had persevered through the absolute hardest season of my entire life, and quite possibly the hardest season I will ever walk through for the rest of my life. But I made it. The light was at the end of the tunnel.

I can tell you with absolute certainty that I did not make it by my own accord. It was nothing more than the grace of God that saw me through that season. I found myself, for the first time in a long time, being able to say with confidence that I was complete. I could not stop the tears from coming as I embraced the beauty of that truth. I was whole. By all measures of earthly standards, it makes no sense to say in that moment that I was complete. But that is because I was not looking at things from an earthly, physical perspective. I was looking at them as Paul describes in 2 Corinthians 4:18, "So we fix our eyes not on what is seen, but on what is unseen, since what is seen is temporary, but what is unseen is eternal."

I was complete because God was with me, and I finally understood that God had always been with me. I had embraced the truths of Hebrews 13:5-6 — that God would never leave me and that He was my helper — as if they were the only life raft that could save me from drowning in the depths of the ocean. I knew He was the only one who could see me through that season. I found joy, even while also experiencing enormous grief, that makes no sense apart from Christ, but with Him, I could trust that James was right. I could surrender the rest of my story to the Lord and

TWELVE

lay it at His feet, knowing that He was going to finish the work He started. I was still a work in progress at that time. He is still not finished with me, even now. But I could relinquish control and know that He is only making me stronger in the process.

As I walked through those few years, I constantly stopped and took a life assessment of God working in and around me. I had to continue walking through the storm. But I continually saw His fingerprints in my life and the lives of those around me. He reminded me throughout that time that He was not going anywhere. He was not going to let guilt and shame be the theme of my life. He was not going to let the enemy silence me out of fear of judgment for this season I found myself in, and this identity I felt like I wore as a sign branded on my forehead. No, He poured out His love over me.

Romans 5:3-5 says:

> Not only so, but we also glory in our sufferings, because we know that suffering produces perseverance; perseverance, character; and character, hope. And hope does not put us to shame, because God's love has been poured out into our hearts through the Holy Spirit, who has been given to us.

I would never wish upon anyone what all three of us in our little family went through at that time. I sat across the table from a dear friend who was walking through a similar journey to mine. She looked at me and said, "Welcome to the club that no one wants to be in, but God moves mightily in."

Divorce is, quite honestly, the one particular thing I prayed against as a child. I have lived through multiple divorces. I never wanted to know what that was like as a spouse. I most certainly never wanted my child to experience what I did growing up. And if I am being honest, I think I had taken on a very judgmental and hypocritical view of why divorce takes place, even within Christianity, before the last few years. However, on the other side of this journey, I have seen and experienced why God hates divorce (Malachi 2:16). I have also seen why, as outlined in Scripture, He would allow divorce to take place under certain circumstances.

Divorce is the death of a marriage. There I was in a place where I had just experienced this death. Two had become one and had been stripped apart to one again. It had not taken place without monumental pain and turmoil. And yet I was finally starting to see the restoration of my soul. The forest of my life had burned to the ground, but the new growth was peeking out from the blackened remains.

I was craving water. I was craving sunlight. I needed nourishment to be able to stand again. But God was providing me with all that I needed at that very moment. A new story and a new journey began to emerge that I was not sure I wanted to embrace, but I came to see it could be beautiful in its own right. God was not done writing my story.

I know far too well that this new chapter is not going to be easy. It will come with its struggles and difficulties. But I know God has a plan through it all, and His glory is that plan. As I continue to turn to Him in each moment, He will continue to meet me in my darkest places and bring light and life to them. He is not leaving me in a desolate place with no chance of survival. He is melting away the resin to plant seeds that will allow for new life to grow.

TWELVE

What an incredible God we have, that He wastes absolutely nothing in our lives. Whatever circumstances you have found yourself in, lay it at the foot of the cross.

Perhaps it was something that was beyond your control that happened to you. It may seem like it is something that God could not possibly use for His glory. First, I want to express my sincerest apologies. For whatever has happened to you that has left you feeling hurt, lost, abandoned, or whatever else it may be, I am sorry. Take some time to read the story of Joseph. Find hope in the message of his life that he summarizes in Genesis 50:20 by saying, "You intended to harm me, but God intended it for good to accomplish what is now being done, the saving of many lives."

Or maybe it has been your own choice to turn away from God and choose to walk in a path of sin. Perhaps that sin has finally reared its ugly head and shown you that it is going to leave you with nothing more than a gaping void. Find hope in the plea of David in Psalm 51:10-12 in response to the sin in his own life, "Create in me a pure heart, O God, and renew a steadfast spirit within me. Do not cast me from your presence or take your Holy Spirit from me. Restore to me the joy of your salvation and grant me a willing spirit, to sustain me."

Hope in the Lord alone. He is unchanging. His love is unconditional. He is always faithful.

I still remember the first time I heard this song by Shane and Shane. I will not lie, I was mad at them for writing it. Why anyone would want to worship God through a song about Him allowing them to be torn down was beyond my comprehension. But in the past few years, this song

"THOUGH YOU SLAY ME"

has become an anthem of my heart. Take a moment to pause and listen to the words of "Though You Slay Me" by Shane and Shane.

I pray wherever you find yourself today that you find hope in these truths of the unchanging character of God.

- *You may feel overcome by fear or feel completely alone, but you can rest in the One who is faithful to keep His promises.*
- *Even though you may feel as if you are being slain, God is on your side, and He is all you need.*

God sees you. God hears you. God loves you.

Chapter 3

"Goodness of God"

Exodus 34:6 says, "And he passed in front of Moses, proclaiming, 'The Lord, the Lord, the compassionate and gracious God, slow to anger, abounding in love and faithfulness.'"

Amidst the upheaval in my personal life, in the spring of 2022, I was informed that the next school year, I would be teaching freshmen Bible rather than senior Bible, as I had for the previous four years. To be honest, I struggled with the change because I knew I could not spend my summer preparing for and creating a new curriculum with as much dedication as I prefer to put into my classes. I knew that throughout the summer, my focus needed to be on my son and myself.

The Lord knew that during that school year, I would need to dive deep into His Word in the moments when my son was not with me. That time forced me to rely on Jesus in moments of anguish rather than turning to unhealthy coping mechanisms or falling into depression. Can you tell

TWELVE

that I am just constantly in awe of how God provides us opportunities to embrace His presence if we will just grab His extended hand and say yes? Because I am.

That transition in positions meant I would be transitioning from teaching apologetics to teaching an Old Testament survey class. I want to emphasize the importance of God's sovereignty during this season. As much as I am passionate about sharing with people why I believe what I believe, God knew that I believed. I knew that I believed. He put me in a place where I spent a year slowing down and focusing solely on Him, sharing Him with ninety-six precious souls. That is honestly what I needed to be reminded of in that particular year to be more prepared to share Him with even more grit, compassion, and empathy than I had before.

Remember the girl who has a hard time trusting people? Remember how I told you that trust in the Lord grows when you dwell with Him? Much to my surprise, the Lord took me on an in-depth journey through the Old Testament to remind me that He is exactly as Exodus 34:6 says, "The Lord, the Lord, the compassionate and gracious God, slow to anger, abounding in love and faithfulness."

I made it a point to discuss every single book of the Old Testament in my classes, even if just for a couple of days. I developed a deeper love for the Lord during that season, as we were all reminded of God's abundant patience and compassion for sinful, selfish, and broken humanity. I kept seeing so much of myself in the Israelites, and I found myself rejoicing in the fact that God is the same today as He was in the past.

"GOODNESS OF GOD"

I decided to study Exodus in-depth throughout that year in my personal, quality time with God. Exodus is such an amazing book of the Old Testament that, if I am being honest, I saw it really as just distant stories from the past up until that year. I began to truly see that the gospel is laid out so clearly in the story of Exodus.

The exodus event is a story of redemption. God rescued the Israelites from slavery in the land of Egypt, but that rescue necessitated a blood sacrifice, a substitute (Exodus 12). Through the sacrifice of the spotless lamb, God granted liberation, and He reconciled the Israelites' relationship with Him. Their trust and faith in God's ability to do what only He can do, in the way He allowed for their rescue to take place, enabled the rest of the events of the exodus to unfold. God established the Mosaic covenant to display His great love. His desire was for the Israelites to experience His incomparable love and reciprocate by showing that same love to a watching world around them. God established the priesthood we often think of when we think back to the Old Testament, which led to deeper communion and reverence for the Lord among the Israelites. All of it led to an intimate relationship with God and a promise of a land to come that would flow with milk and honey.

If you need a reminder of what Christ accomplished for us on the cross and the great lengths God has gone to make it possible for us to know and live in His love, take some time to read through the entire book of Exodus.

But do you know what is astounding?! God rescued them from slavery by some of the most drastic means possible, the ten plagues, that only the people living on earth during that time and the time some of the

TWELVE

events in Revelation will take place will ever understand (Exodus 7-11). *THEN* He provided a pillar of cloud by day and a pillar of fire by night to continue to guide the people (Exodus 13). *THEN* He parted the Red Sea for the Israelites to cross on dry ground and wiped away the Egyptian army pursuing after them (Exodus 14). *THEN* they shared a beautiful song of admiration and praise for who God was to them and all He had done for those who were faithful to hear His offering of grace and respond (Exodus 15).

Let's pause here for just a moment before continuing with the events of the exodus. Read through this song of praise slowly and maybe even two or three times.

Exodus 15:1-18 says:

Then Moses and the Israelites sang this song to the Lord:

I will sing to the Lord, for he is highly exalted.

Both horse and driver he has hurled into the sea.

The Lord is my strength and my defense; he has become my salvation.

He is my God, and I will praise him, my father's God, and I will exalt him.

The Lord is a warrior; the Lord is his name.

Pharaoh's chariots and his army he has hurled into the sea.

The best of Pharaoh's officers are drowned in the Red Sea.

The deep waters have covered them; they sank to the depths like a stone.

Your right hand, Lord, was majestic in power.

Your right hand, Lord, shattered the enemy.

"GOODNESS OF GOD"

In the greatness of your majesty you threw down those who opposed you.

You unleashed your burning anger; it consumed them like stubble.

By the blast of your nostrils the waters piled up.

The surging waters stood up like a wall; the deep waters congealed in the heart of the sea.

The enemy boasted, 'I will pursue, I will overtake them.

I will divide the spoils; I will gorge myself on them.

I will draw my sword and my hand will destroy them.'

But you blew with your breath, and the sea covered them.

They sank like lead in the mighty waters.

Who among the gods is like you, Lord?

Who is like you—majestic in holiness, awesome in glory, working wonders?

You stretch out your right hand, and the earth swallows your enemies.

In your unfailing love you will lead the people you have redeemed.

In your strength you will guide them to your holy dwelling.

The nations will hear and tremble; anguish will grip the people of Philistia.

The chiefs of Edom will be terrified, the leaders of Moab will be seized with trembling, the people of Canaan will melt away; terror and dread will fall on them.

By the power of your arm they will be as still as a stone—until your people pass by, Lord, until the people you bought pass by.

TWELVE

> You will bring them in and plant them on the mountain of your inheritance—the place, Lord, you made for your dwelling, the sanctuary, Lord, your hands established.
>
> The Lord reigns for ever and ever.

Now, let's continue. THEN... and this is the astounding part... somehow following that incredible moment of worship, the Israelites complained about their lack of water (Exodus 15:24). *THEN* they grumbled about their lack of food (Exodus 16:2). In both instances, it is clear that they even doubted God's ability to provide them with water and food. From that point forward, the grumbling was continual.

God provided food and water. God provided shelter. But more than that, God provided Himself. Even after seeing and living through slavery, the ten plagues, the pillars of cloud and fire, and the parting of the Red Sea, the very same people had forgotten the heart of God. He did not rescue them from slavery to abandon them in the desert. However, as you continue through Exodus and the rest of the Old Testament, you see that it never changes. Somehow, following the moment of crying out in praise to a God who they saw work these miraculous events to rescue them, they chose to distance themselves from Him and remain far from Him.

By the time you get to Numbers 32, you see that they are unconvinced of God's great power and plan for them. That doubt came at a cost. God told them that for their lack of faith, they would have to spend forty years wandering in the desert, which was long enough for everyone in the generation of those who had gone to scope out the promised land to die, except Joshua and Caleb, because they had unwavering faith in God and His ability to keep His promises.

"GOODNESS OF GOD"

Here was God rescuing them, adopting them as His people, and sharing a plan of complete restoration; yet, here were people hearing God's plan to love and care for them, and yet they chose to turn away. Instead of remaining in that place of worship, they cried out, saying they wished they had died in Egypt or, at the very least, they wanted to return to Egypt (Exodus 16:3, Numbers 14:4).

I am sorry, but what?! Who in their right mind says, "God, thank you for all you have done. I mean, you saved me and my family, particularly my firstborn son, and my people, and even people from Egypt who also had faith and came with us, but I am just not sure you can feed me. I think I will go back."

Exodus 34:6 says, "And he passed in front of Moses, proclaiming, 'The Lord, the Lord, the compassionate and gracious God, slow to anger, abounding in love and faithfulness.'" I mean, if you did not believe God was truly compassionate, gracious, slow to anger, and abounding in love and faithfulness before, imagine, just imagine being in His place for this particular event. I mean, really. When I do something so minimal and my son forgets to thank me, I remind him to be grateful. Of course, that is a whole lot more about cultivating a heart of gratitude in his life, but it is also nice to be appreciated now and then. Can you just imagine being in the place of God at that very moment?

At first glance, the Israelites are nothing short of mind-boggling. Well, let us not be so quick to point fingers, as I naturally want to do when reading through this event.

When I started planning this trip back in December 2022, I was overwhelmed with excitement from the very beginning. What I would

TWELVE

naturally think would lead me to an overwhelming feeling of fear and trembling just did not, for some reason.

As time went on and more friends and family found out about my trip, fear was the predominant response. I could see in their faces a deep desire to support this prompting of the Lord and a willing heart to follow through with it, but I could also clearly see that they thought I had lost my mind.

In the kindest of ways, many people asked if there was anyone who could join me. I ended up asking a few friends if they wanted to join, but the timing did not work with any of their schedules. I was honestly relieved when each shared that they could not go, as I had felt sure this was something I needed to do on my own, but I also wanted to heed wise counsel. I had several friends look me in the eyes and say, "You are right. You need to do this. I think you are going to love it."

Then, leading up to the actual trip, numerous obstacles started to appear. Days before I was supposed to leave, my mom had a surgery unexpectedly scheduled for the middle of my journey, and I wanted to be there to help her. Some friends asked if our son wanted to play in a soccer tournament, and I wanted to watch him play in it as well. Both of those were great things I could have done. But as I prayed, I kept coming back to feeling positively sure that this trip was where the Lord wanted me to invest my time that particular week.

Little did I know that God's timing could not have been more deliberate. One day, perhaps I will no longer be so surprised by God's intimate knowledge of what is to come, but for some reason, it always blows my mind how He works. In His sovereignty, a trip I had planned seven months earlier was scheduled for the day after we filed for divorce. I had lunch with a dear friend and mentor that day, after we had both signed and submitted the divorce papers. Emotions inundated me from all different sides. It was very much like a scene from *Inside Out,* with all of the different characters battling for their turn to control the switchboard. But she looked at me and said, "Amber, there is one thing you can rest assured of. God is with you. He loves you. His timing is sweet. And I cannot wait to hear how He continues to show you that over this next week."

The next morning, I finished loading my car and went to open the garage door to pull out of my home in Oklahoma and begin the journey North. But then the unthinkable happened. A wire in my garage door snapped, and it would not open. My garage door had just had this issue a few weeks prior. I had just had it repaired. How it happened again makes no logical sense, except that it makes perfect sense when you factor in that this is something God wanted me to do. I manually opened the garage door, pulled my car out, and then manually closed it, deciding I would deal with the issue at another time. Off I went.

Within just a couple of hours of driving, I found myself driving through the windiest, craziest storm I have ever driven in while going through Kansas. There was an absolute downpour of rain, filled with some decent-sized hail and winds that made it almost impossible to stay in my lane. I prayed the hail would not break my windshield, and I tried to just take it one mile at a time. I saw multiple cars stuck on the side of the road, and even a few semis had flipped over due to the wind.

When I passed through the storm, it was almost as if it were a metaphor for my life. I had physically passed through the storm, but I had

TWELVE

also emotionally and spiritually passed through a storm. The Lord had seen me through it all. I was on dry ground again. Now I was ready for complete healing and restoration to happen. In an instant, I moved from a place of fear of the unknown in the future to a place of expectancy for what the Lord had ahead.

When I arrived at my campsite at Jenny Lake Campground at Grand Teton National Park the next night, I found myself reflecting on Exodus. I read through the notes I had taken on Exodus, and then sat in silence for a bit.

There were parts of 2022 when I had cried out to God, asking Him to just go back in time to where my prayers consisted of a longing for Vancouver and a finalized adoption. I did not want to hurt so badly. I did not want to see my son hurt so badly. The destruction that took place touched every part of my heart, and it was awful. James 1 was a struggle to believe in that season. I will not sugarcoat it one bit. I had to stop and either say out loud or write down how I saw God working to muster up the strength to press on for another day. I wanted to go backward in time. But then I would read my journals from the previous years and know I did not want to go backwards because I did not want to forget all He had done. God knew what was going to come out of that season was going to be far more beautiful than whatever I thought beautiful was supposed to look like in my life.

Hear me loud and clear, I was not in a place of slavery like the Israelites. That is not at all what I am saying. It was painfully obvious those years from the past were not ones I wanted to relive, but not because I felt enslaved. Why would I ever want to go back to that place after I had seen

"GOODNESS OF GOD"

God work in miraculous ways and move metaphorical mountains to show Himself to me throughout that year? Why would I ever want to forget this undeniable evidence of God's presence in my life? The truth was, I did not want to forget. I did not want to go back.

As I sat there reflecting on Exodus and my tendency to respond like the Israelites, I reminded myself of God's goodness. He was undeniably at work. He was providing all I needed. He had been and always would be faithful. I just needed to keep taking the next step, trusting Him to go before me. I reminded myself that He will never stop leading me as long as I keep my eyes fixed on Him and follow Him. He truly is so good, loving, and kind. He has always been, and He will always be.

I knew in the days ahead, He was going to show that to be true. He was going to show me that I was safe to lay down the broken pieces of my life. He was going to put them together again. I could surrender it all to Him because I knew He only wanted what was best for me to grow into more of Christ every day.

So that is what I prayed for that evening. I prayed God would allow me to lay down this new season of life at His feet. By the time I returned home from my trip, I knew our finalized divorce papers would be in my mailbox, and they were indeed. There was no better way for me to shift into this new season than by placing it into His hands and allowing myself to be engrossed in His presence. He is all I wanted. He is most certainly all I needed. That is precisely where I needed to be.

Perhaps you are walking through something difficult, making it hard to see God at work. There may be a sin that has had a foothold in your life for far too long that you need to stop trying to fight on your own

TWELVE

and allow the Lord to step in and help you overcome. There may be an incredibly unhealthy relationship with someone who needs to have some boundaries put in place to best care for and protect your heart. There may be an increasingly difficult relationship with a spouse, family member, or friend that you may need to seek out wise counsel to walk with you and speak into the situation(s) at hand.

There are many places we can walk in life that can feel as if they have enslaved us (or perhaps they truly have enslaved us), some by our own doing and some not by our choice. I pray that if you are in one of those places, you will be willing to open your eyes to the goodness of God and how He is working. I pray you will allow Him to work in it. Let Him into the depths of your heart. Let Him guide you to wise, biblical counsel through whatever means possible to navigate that journey with you.

At times, I have sought out biblical counsel from church leaders, mentors, friends, licensed counselors, and others. God has created us for community, and within that community, He has provided people with incredible gifts to walk alongside one another in those difficult spaces. Let them be a light and speak life into those places. We have to do the hard work of letting our guard down so that God and those He leads us to can actually enter into those difficult experiences with us.

I know it is scary. I know it is hard. And you may very well get hurt because the people we have as brothers and sisters in Christ are just that — brothers and sisters. They are not God Himself. They are not perfect. They are sinners striving to be more like Jesus, and sometimes they fall short of that goal. They are no different than anyone else in that regard. However, that does not mean that one person falling short allows us to ignore God's commands in Scripture to rejoice with others and mourn with them, and vice versa. We need other believers walking with us in all seasons of our lives. We need to be those brothers and sisters willing to walk with others wherever they may be as well. We will revisit this topic later.

But then, after you allow yourself to see God's hand at work, be willing to let that truly resonate in your heart. Let that help you to see God not as some distant being in a faraway place, but instead as your Father and Friend who will not leave your side. There is such a sweetness to seeing Him as Father and Friend together. Each brings about different strengths. As our Father, He is our protector. He loves us unconditionally. He truly wants what is best for us. As our Friend, He is willing to walk with us arm in arm and hand in hand through it all. He is willing to listen. He is willing to help. He is willing to be actively involved. As our Father and our Friend, He is with us in every possible way that we need. He is willing to be present. He is with you. You can trust Him.

This song is one I often turn to as a reminder of who God truly is, which I see so clearly when I look to Him rather than to the world. May we all grow in fixing our eyes upon Jesus, the author and perfecter of our faith (Hebrews 12:1-2). Take a moment to pause and listen to the words of "Goodness of God" by The Worship Initiative.

I pray wherever you find yourself today that you find hope in these truths of the unchanging character of God.

- *You may feel overcome by fear or feel completely alone, but you can rest in the One who is faithful to keep His promises.*

TWELVE

- *Even though you may feel as if you are being slain, God is on your side, and He is all you need.*
- *The goodness of God is all around you and running hard after you.*

God sees you. God hears you. God loves you.

Chapter 4

"Firm Foundation"

Acts 17:26-27 says, "From one man he made all the nations, that they should inhabit the whole earth; and he marked out their appointed times in history and the boundaries of their lands. God did this so that they would seek him and perhaps reach out for him and find him, though he is not far from any one of us."

    When I arrived at Jenny Lake Campground at Grand Teton National Park, this precious lady was at the check-in booth. She informed me that there had been a bear sighting there that day (and for several days before), so I should be bear aware. This bear sighting was not of one bear, but three bears — a momma and her two cubs. I already told you one of my main goals of the trip was not to be mauled by a bear.

    For some strange reason, when I thought that would immediately flood my mind with thoughts of fear, I instead decided right then and there

TWELVE

to sleep with my bear spray and pray that everything would be all right. Thanks to the Lord, I was flooded with peace in that moment.

So, I drove to my campsite, set up my tent, prepared dinner, and retrieved my Bible, journal, and commentary, which I planned to start walking through. I sat there and began to appreciate the beauty of God's creation He had brought me to at the exact moment I needed it. My campsite had a spigot for the water. It was not right by my picnic table or tent, but it was close enough that I could interact with people if I wanted to when they came to get water. Well, that just so happens to be who I am. So, every single person who came to get water, I would say hello and ask how they were doing.

These two men came from the campsite diagonally across from mine and were speaking a language that I could not identify. I asked them where they were from. They informed me they were from Belgium, which is the country I have visited the most in my life outside of the United States and Canada. I was overjoyed to hear they were from Belgium. We discussed what had brought me to Belgium and what had brought them to the United States for a brief period, and then they went their separate ways.

The next evening, one of them came over to my picnic table while I was once again eating dinner and spending time with Jesus, using my Bible, journal, and commentary that I had laid out on my table. He came to show me a video from that morning of the bear and her two cubs, because the bears were roaming throughout both of our campsites. I had left early that morning for a hike. But within about an hour of my departure, there was the momma bear just walking right beside my tent.

"FIRM FOUNDATION"

We were talking about the craziness of wildlife when all of a sudden, he looked down at my open Bible and said, "What is that?" I looked at him, puzzled, and said, "What do you mean, 'What is that?' It's a Bible. Have you ever seen a Bible before?" He then told me he had, but let's just say my Bible is a little like organized chaos. I have one of those journal Bibles that artsy people typically draw beautiful pictures in the margins. I have zero artistic abilities, so rather than drawings, bullet-pointed notes and sticky notes containing additional bullet-pointed notes fill the margins. My handwriting is also just a tad bit unique. The Dean of Students at the university I attended told me throughout college that he was going to make my handwriting his font in his emails. My Bible does look a smidge staggering at first glance.

He said, "I can tell you really like to study your Bible." I responded to him by saying, "Well, I believe this is the Word of God. It is the truth. If I really believe that, I should want to know it. Don't you think so?" He completely agreed.

That led to a lengthy conversation on religion. I learned that this friend grew up in a Muslim family, but some of his siblings had converted to Christianity. He no longer claimed a religion, but he did believe there had to be a Creator. His family could not talk about religion anymore because it just resulted in frustration for everyone involved. As we stood in a place surrounded by the handiwork of God in creation, we recounted to one another all that we believed was true of the Creator.

We agreed that He had to be purposeful to account for the order that is present in the world. Proverbs 16:4 says, "The Lord works out everything to its proper end— even the wicked for a day of disaster." First

TWELVE

Corinthians 14:33 says, "For God is not a God of disorder but of peace—as in all the congregations of the Lord's people."

We agreed that He had to be good to provide all that He did for people. James 1:17 says, "Every good and perfect gift is from above, coming down from the Father of the heavenly lights, who does not change like shifting shadows." Philippians 4:19 says, "And my God will meet all your needs according to the riches of his glory in Christ Jesus."

We agreed that He had to be just and willing to make things right at some point. Psalm 89:14 says, "Righteousness and justice are the foundation of your throne; love and faithfulness go before you." Deuteronomy 32:4 says, "He is the Rock, his works are perfect, and all his ways are just. A faithful God who does no wrong, upright and just is he."

We agreed that He had to be selfless. Matthew 20:28 says, "Just as the Son of Man did not come to be served, but to serve, and to give his life as a ransom for many." John 15:33 says, "Greater love has no one than this: to lay down one's life for one's friends."

We agreed that He had to be the Creator of all people from all ethnicities and love them fully. Genesis 1:27 says, "So God created mankind in his own image, in the image of God he created them; male and female he created them." Revelation 7:9-10 says:

> After this I looked, and there before me was a great multitude that no one could count, from every nation, tribe, people and language, standing before the throne and before the Lamb. They were wearing white robes and were holding palm branches in their hands. And they cried out in a loud voice: "Salvation belongs to our God, who sits on the throne, and to the Lamb."

"FIRM FOUNDATION"

We agreed that He had to love all people and want all people to experience His love. First Timothy 2:4-6 says:

> Who wants all people to be saved and to come to a knowledge of the truth. For there is one God and one mediator between God and mankind, the man Christ Jesus, who gave himself as a ransom for all people. This has now been witnessed to at the proper time.

Second Peter 3:9 says, "The Lord is not slow in keeping his promise, as some understand slowness. Instead, he is patient with you, not wanting anyone to perish, but everyone to come to repentance."

We agreed that He had to be intentional. Acts 17:26-27 says:

> From one man he made all the nations, that they should inhabit the whole earth; and he marked out their appointed times in history and the boundaries of their lands. God did this so that they would seek him and perhaps reach out for him and find him, though he is not far from any one of us.

Ephesians 2:10 says, "For we are God's handiwork, created in Christ Jesus to do good works, which God prepared in advance for us to do."

It even led us to agree that there was no way on earth that we came from two very different places and happened to be in the same place at the same time, and that we were having the conversation by chance. As we talked, I flipped through my Bible, discussing how all that we agreed on is exactly as God is described in the Bible from Genesis to Revelation. That will forever be one of my favorite conversations with someone outside of the Christian faith. It was sweet to see someone believe everything about who they imagined God to be, not realizing that is exactly how He is described in the Bible, because that is who He is. I do not know if that

TWELVE

friend will ever come to know Jesus as his personal Lord and Savior. I continue to pray that he does.

After he left my campsite, I started reading through my Bible. I had just started going through Hebrews the night before. Hebrews is one of the most confusing books of the New Testament if you do not have a good foundational understanding of the Old Testament. However, after teaching through the Old Testament for a year and participating in an in-depth study of Exodus, I knew that I wanted to study Hebrews next. There I sat reading through Hebrews.

Hebrews 2:1-4 says:

We must pay the most careful attention, therefore, to what we have heard, so that we do not drift away. For since the message spoken through angels was binding, and every violation and disobedience received its just punishment, how shall we escape if we ignore so great a salvation? This salvation, which was first announced by the Lord, was confirmed to us by those who heard him. God also testified to it by signs, wonders and various miracles, and by gifts of the Holy Spirit distributed according to his will.

I had just flipped through numerous passages throughout Scripture as this friend and I recounted the character of God. Then, reading Hebrews 2:1-4, I was reminded of how much we continually need to speak those truths to ourselves. Remembering God's unchanging character strengthens our faith. God is constantly faithful throughout all generations. That is never going to change.

At that particular moment, I realized that God had been faithful throughout my entire journey. I found myself in a place where I was stuck in a dichotomy of believing God was there and had been there all along, while also feeling like He might not be there after all. I was struggling to have faith that He would continue to work in and through me in this new season.

In 2022, I had to battle numerous lies that came my way from a few people; those lies were also directly dispelled by many other people. But words are hard to forget, even when you know they are not true. Proverbs 18:21 says, "The tongue has the power of life and death, and those who love it will eat its fruit." I had been so sure of who God was and that I knew His voice because it was only because of Him that I made it through that season. He had prepared my heart for every single thing that came my way in the spring of 2022 before it ever came to fruition. But others had tried to convince me that it was not Him.

I do want to be clear about what I mean. I have never heard an audible voice like Morgan Freeman's speaking in my head. What I have heard is a voice within me that sounds like my own voice but shares truths that align with God's Word, sometimes directly from God's Word. Most of the time, it is in a moment of feeling overwhelmed and anxious that the Lord brings specific Scriptures to mind. Sometimes it is Him speaking directly to a situation, reminding me to hold onto Him and trust Him. Sometimes it is Him revealing to me a glimpse of what is to come, even though I may not understand it at the moment. Sometimes it is a prompt to reach out and ask someone if they are doing okay, or to stop and pray for someone at that moment, even if I do not know why.

Here is an example. We received our referral for the precious boy we were in the process of adopting in November of 2021. In March of 2022,

TWELVE

we received an email with his pictures. I was sitting in our school's basketball gym, surrounded by our leadership students. We were eating lunch, preparing for our final assembly after a week filled with assemblies and events in support of a local, faith-based organization in our city. We were exhausted. We were already emotional. For the first time, I gazed upon this sweet child's little eyes and at his adorable face. That should have been a moment of overwhelming joy.

Instead, I opened the email, not realizing exactly what it contained, and started weeping. All of my students looked at me, trying to figure out what was going on. I ran to the restroom to wipe away my tears and collect my thoughts. When I came back out, all I said to them was that we had just received pictures of our little boy. What I did not tell them was that the moment I looked into his eyes, the Lord made it very clear to me that I was not looking into the eyes of my child. I could not tell you why then, but I knew beyond a shadow of a doubt that he was not going to be coming home to our family. I shared that with a friend later that evening. The Lord's voice had been so clear to me, and just a few weeks later, we would find out we were not going to be able to bring him home.

John 10:27-30 says:

My sheep listen to my voice; I know them, and they follow me. I give them eternal life, and they shall never perish; no one will snatch them out of my hand. My Father, who has given them to me, is greater than all; no one can snatch them out of my Father's hand. I and the Father are one.

I knew God's voice then. I know it now. He is sweet to walk with us throughout our days and be with us, prompting us to be obedient in loving and serving others and encouraging us to draw near to Him. That season, He continually made Himself known to me in a way that I could not have even articulated how much I needed. In a season where I felt exceedingly helpless, I never felt hopeless because I knew He was with me.

That moment talking with that friend at Jenny Lake reminded me that God was still walking with me. I did not have to doubt His love for me. I did not have to doubt His presence in me. He was not going anywhere. He had perfectly planned out this time for me to remember just that. Romans 8:38-39 says:

> For I am convinced that neither death nor life, neither angels nor demons, neither the present nor the future, nor any powers, neither height nor depth, nor anything else in all creation, will be able to separate us from the love of God that is in Christ Jesus our Lord.

If you are in a place where the Lord has been convicting you of your sin, listen to that conviction. Do not run from Him. Run to Him. Let Him catch you, hold you, and set you free from whatever has you entangled.

If you are in a place where the Lord has been prompting you to go and share with someone, be willing to walk in obedience even with fear and trembling, and do it! He will provide you with everything you need to accomplish what He has ahead for you.

If you are in a place where the Lord has placed a desire to go and have that hard conversation with someone to take responsibility for your actions and apologize, do it. I know it is hard. I know it is humbling. I know it is challenging to expect nothing in return and receive nothing in return from those moments, but that is not why God asks you to do it anyway. He

TWELVE

is teaching you and growing you more in that moment than you will ever even know.

If you are in a place where God is leading you to confront someone else about their sin and how it is affecting you, approach the conversation as gently as possible and have that conversation. This might be the most challenging conversation of all. I understand that place. I have been there more than once. It is terrifying not knowing what someone else's response may be. But at the end of the day, remember that you are being a vessel of love and grace to that person.

You are never responsible for anyone else's response to any of the above, but you are always responsible for being obedient to what God is asking you to do. No matter how others respond, you are safe with Him. He is unchanging. He will continue to be with you through the most difficult of storms. Keep listening for Him. Keep looking for Him. Keep walking in faith.

Remember that the Lord has created you to be present in the time and place that you are right now. He has a purpose for you. As long as you are holding tightly to Him, nothing can shake you. No matter what storms may come, your house will stand. The walls may shake and feel like they will give way, but if the Lord is where your strength lies, then no storm will be able to overtake you. You can rest assured that He can help you withstand anything that comes your way.

I recall a distinct Sunday when we sang "Firm Foundation" in church during worship. I am not typically a crier during worship. I usually have a smile on my face during worship, out of gratitude for being able to worship the God who, for some reason, has chosen to love me, even though I am keenly aware that I do not deserve it. But on that particular Sunday in the spring of 2022, we sang "Firm Foundation." As soon as we got to the bridge, I lost it.

Rain came, wind blew

But my house was built on You

I'm safe with You

I'm gonna make it through

I did not feel safe at that moment. I did not feel safe to feel what I was feeling. I did not feel safe saying what I felt needed to be said. I felt like my house was caving in from every direction in my life. It felt as if the floor was going to give way at any given moment. But I sang that song, and as tears streamed down my face, I prayed for the Lord to remind me that I was safe with Him continually. He was going to help me make it through.

Now there I sat in Wyoming in the summer of 2023, recounting God's faithfulness. I was reading about the importance of holding tightly to that truth so that I do not drift away, and the next thing I knew, I found myself turning on "Firm Foundation." I began praying this song as the cry of my heart in that moment to remember that He was an unmovable rock I could stand on. He was not going to fail me. He was never going to abandon me. He will not fail you either. Take a moment to pause and listen to the words of "Firm Foundation" by Cody Carnes.

I pray wherever you find yourself today that you find hope in these truths of the unchanging character of God.

- *You may feel overcome by fear or feel completely alone, but you can rest in the One who is faithful to keep His promises.*

TWELVE

- *Even though you may feel as if you are being slain, God is on your side, and He is all you need.*
- *The goodness of God is all around you and running hard after you.*
- *God is a firm foundation on which you can stand; you are safe with Him.*

God sees you. God hears you. God loves you.

Chapter 5

"I'm Listening"

Jeremiah 33:3 says, "Call to me and I will answer you and tell you great and unsearchable things you do not know."

I had a student tell me that while I was at Grand Teton National Park, I had to do the Phelps Lake Trail. She told me it was her and her family's favorite hike they did while there. So, of course, I put that trail on my list. I woke up early one morning to the sound of chirping birds surrounded by the absolute best, crisp mountain air. I made my morning tea, ate breakfast, and headed to the trailhead. This was the morning the momma bear went on a bit of a morning stroll through my campsite. It was early enough that there were only two other cars in the parking lot when I got there.

That morning was, hands down, the most peaceful and serene hike I have ever been on in my life. Until the last hour, I saw a total of three people on that hike. The pictures you see of the crystal-clear reflections of

TWELVE

the mountain onto the lake water were exactly what that hike consisted of for the most part. It also had the most peaceful running water through the creeks and the absolute best lookout points, offering a stunning view back over the lake with the mountains on one side and trees for miles on the other.

But my very favorite spot of the hike was a field of wildflowers. It was full of every possible color. I am not even exaggerating when I say that I danced in the wildflowers. I simply could not contain the joy of seeing the vibrant blue, red, purple, and yellow flowers all around me, waving in the cool breeze. It was easily one of my favorite moments of the trip.

While I was on that hike, since there was no one around, I had my worship music playing all morning. Whoever "they" are says that you should make noise so that wild animals (bears and moose, particularly) hear you coming and can flee before you even cross paths with them. Well, I was not about to just talk to myself all day long, though I would not put that past me. Instead, I had music playing while I walked along the edge of the lake, enjoying every single moment of that hike.

I took time to stop and reflect in the many lovely places I came across while hiking. Those are some of my favorite moments. I am a deep thinker. I assume you have gathered that by now, though. My mind constantly wanders to many different places. It was sweet to sit in the stillness of the mountains and gaze upon God's beautiful creation.

As I hiked along the lake that day, I kept coming back to 1 Corinthians 14:33, which says, "For God is not a God of disorder but of peace—as in all the congregations of the Lord's people." Some translations use the term "confusion" instead of "disorder." I had lived in a place of confusion for a long time. I had felt like disorder was all around me for a couple of years. Over the several months leading up to that trip, I felt increasingly the peace of God surrounding me. The Lord had constantly reminded me that He is not a God of confusion.

I was seeing clearly for the first time in a while. I was able to step back from life and look at what had transpired from a 10,000-foot view, rather than being overwhelmed by the forest that seemed to be surrounding me. It was like the fog that had overtaken my thoughts was finally subsiding, and the sun was coming out clear as day. I had hoped that it would take place by removing distractions, and I was thankful that it genuinely did.

One of my favorite things to do when I was teaching in the classroom was to start every class period with a "Question of the Day." My students grew to love it even more than I did. However, the primary purpose was to ask random questions to get more to the heart of the students and know what they enjoyed, what they did not like, and build camaraderie and community in the classroom to promote class discussions. I am also naturally a connector. I strive to find something I can connect with every person on, which is much easier than you might think. I have found that there are students who hate pickles as much as I do, cannot touch cotton balls like me, and who love concerts as much as I do.

One of my favorite questions was to ask, "If you had to lose one of your five senses, which would you give up and why?" Never was someone willing to surrender vision or hearing. Taste and smell were the two most common answers. Touch was a rare occurrence. However, when it came

TWELVE

to hearing and vision, there was no chance anyone was willing to give those up. Why?

Well, the two are intrinsically linked to one another. The ability to see and hear changes everything about our experiences of every moment of our lives. Not only that, but they are truly linked together in how our brain processes through our nerve pathways.

I have never struggled with hearing, but I have had a lifelong challenge with my vision. When I was in third grade, I was playing basketball at school when our coach told me to pass the ball to a specific girl on my team. I still distinctly remember that moment. I looked down the court, and everyone looked the same. They were all blurry figures moving around. I asked him which one she was, and he quickly realized I was not kidding. Soon after, I was taken to the eye doctor and given a pair of glasses. In sixth grade, I attempted (attempted might even be a stretch) to play volleyball, but my glasses kept falling off my face and breaking. So, I started wearing contacts.

For over twenty-five years, my eyesight at times would get worse (to the point that I was considered legally blind for several years), and then unexpectedly get a little better. But even on the best day, I could only see well about 4-5 inches in front of my face. After that, it was all one blurry mess.

Then flash forward to April 2022. In April of 2022, I ran the half-marathon at the Oklahoma City Memorial Marathon. Following the marathon, I went to two graduation parties for six of my seniors. I noticed throughout the day, in pictures, that something was wrong with my right eye. It was really puffy. It almost looked like I had had an allergic reaction to something.

Over the next couple of months, the swelling in that eye would occasionally subside, but it never returned to its normal state. Then it would swell right back up again. Finally, in September 2022, I visited the eye doctor. That then led to nine months of me trying different medications and having tests to figure out what in the world was going on with my body.

It started with steroid eye drops for several weeks, which then led to me taking oral steroids as well. When that did not help, my doctor recommended that I go a few weeks without wearing contacts. When that did not have any effect, my doctor recommended that I see an ophthalmologist. The ophthalmologist had me start with blood work to ensure my thyroid levels, among many other things, were fine. Thankfully, that all came back clear. Then words began being said that a newly single mom does not want to hear. My doctor recommended I have an MRI to be sure it was not a brain tumor, a symptom of a potential stroke or brain aneurysm, or some other kind of neurological issue.

I had never had an MRI before, but let me tell you that an MRI of your head is next level. The helmet you have to wear is utterly terrifying. I sat there with my eyes closed, trying hard to focus on the Ellie Holcomb Pandora music I had requested, which felt like it could have turned up about twenty notches to at least a somewhat audible level over the insanity of sound that is the MRI machine. But I made it through, and the results were clear (praise Jesus!). Next, my doctor referred me to an ENT

TWELVE

specialist to undergo a CT scan. The CT scan came back clear. My doctor then referred me to an oculoplastic surgeon.

In June 2023, I sat in the chair of the oculoplastic surgeon's office, honestly, at a point of just accepting that there was no explanation for what was happening, and I was just going to have to deal with it. But she walked in and said, "I know you feel like you've been on a never-ending search to figure out what's wrong with your eye. Even if you had come straight to me, I would have done all of the same tests ahead of time. But good news, I think I know exactly what is wrong." She put some drops in my right eye, left for ten minutes, and came back. She asked if I had looked in a mirror, which I had not, nor did I know I had any reason to at that moment. She raised a mirror in front of my face, and all of a sudden, my right eye looked completely normal, but my left eye looked swollen. She then proceeded to tell me she knew exactly what was wrong and how to fix it.

However, there was one aspect that confused her. The doctor said I had nerve damage in both eyes that was causing my muscles to weaken, but my right eye was worse than my left eye. What was strange was that everything about my eyes, blood work, neurological tests, and so on, came back perfectly normal. She looked at me and said, "You are young and happy and healthy. The only thing I can even think of that could cause this would be immense stress, but that just does not make sense."

I assured her that that indeed made sense and timeline-wise added up perfectly. April 2022 was the peak of the stress hitting. When "they" say immense stress can cause some damage to your body, "they" are not kidding. It is quite destructive. But the good news was she also knew exactly what to do to correct it. My doctor recommended that I have some type of vision correction surgery completed before the surgery on the nerves and muscles in my eyes to eliminate the need for contacts and glasses that could cause additional stress and strain on my eyes.

After I spent years of my childhood being embarrassed by my glasses and then years of sitting on the bathroom countertop crying because it took me so long to be able to put my contacts in and take them out (now I can do it in a second without even needing a mirror), I had vision correction surgery. I never would have had the surgery, but I wanted to do all I could to prevent the other issues in my eyes from resurfacing.

Now I know what it is like to open your eyes in the morning after waking up and be able to see everything. For days, I would try to take my contacts out at night and reach for my glasses in the morning. But each time, I found myself getting emotional about the fact that I could now see. It is a moving experience to see clearly for the first time in your life without the aid of glasses or contacts.

I'm writing this from the comfort of my couch following the subsequent surgery I had to have in this healing process on my eyes. Yesterday I had surgery to repair the nerves and muscles in my eyes. I spent yesterday and today following this exact routine repeatedly.

(Place frozen peas on my eyes.)

Me: "Alexa, set a thirty-minute timer."

Alexa: "Thirty minutes starting now."

(Timer goes off.)

Me: "Alexa, restart the thirty-minute timer."

(Remove frozen peas from my eyes and place them in the freezer.)

TWELVE

Repeat. Repeat. Repeat.

Except, if I'm being honest, it is more like this.

(Place frozen peas on my eyes.)

Me: "Alexa, set a thirty-minute timer."

Alexa: "Thirty minutes starting now."

Me: "Alexa, how much time is left?"

Alexa: "You have twenty-three minutes left of your thirty-minute timer."

Me: "Alexa, how much time is left?"

Alexa: "You have sixteen minutes left of your thirty-minute timer."

(Timer goes off.)

Me: "Alexa, restart the thirty-minute timer."

(Remove frozen peas from eyes and place in the freezer. Then spend thirty minutes doing anything but lying down with frozen peas on my eyes.)

As I write this, I am in one of my thirty-minute breaks from frozen peas, and I am so very thankful for the reprieve. As obnoxious as yesterday, today, and tomorrow will be, I am grateful for the in-depth understanding of our bodies God has given us. The gift of medicine, which enables us to treat our bodies, is precisely that, a gift.

When I hiked the Phelps Lake Trail, one thought that kept coming back to me was that God was providing healing in many parts of my being. God, in His grace, had provided answers and the method He would use to heal the physical ailments that had begun to surface during such a taxing season on my body. But He was also going to touch and restore me and my story in every other way as well.

Some scars are most certainly going to remain, physically and emotionally. There are parts of the story where the healing will ultimately only come through entering the gates of Heaven, but healing will come nonetheless. Jeremiah 33:3 says, "Call to me and I will answer you and tell you great and unsearchable things you do not know."

In a season when I felt like my vision was metaphorically and physically fading, all I knew to do was cry out to God. Not only is our vision and hearing directly linked in our physical body, but there is also a spiritual link. I did not understand how and why the hard things just kept piling up. Was it ever going to come to a stopping point? I really was not sure. But God kept reminding me that He was going to show me things I could not have learned any other way. He was going to take me deeper than I had ever gone with Him before. But to get there, I had to be willing to listen to Him and for Him. I had to be willing to quiet my fears, worries and thoughts. As I did that, He would help me see Him moving.

I had to be still in His presence.

That is what I did that day at Phelps Lake Trail. I called on Him, believing with all of my heart that He would answer me. I knew He wanted to show me great and unsearchable things in that moment and throughout my time away, but that was only going to happen if I turned toward Him.

He continually reminds me that I learn the most by simply being still and listening. I am still a work in progress on James 1:19, but I am constantly praying to be better and better at following the wisdom James shared in that passage, "My dear brothers and sisters, take note of this:

TWELVE

Everyone should be quick to listen, slow to speak and slow to become angry."

As the fog began to clear from my perspective on that day, I found myself seeing life as Elisha did in 2 Kings 6. God had given Elisha a vision that the king of Aram was going to come and attack Israel. The king of Aram did not appreciate Elisha's warning, so he instead set out to capture Elisha. Elisha's servant became quite fearful, probably for good reason, when he saw the Arameans coming to attack them.

But one of my favorite moments of Scripture takes place in 2 Kings 6:16, "'Don't be afraid,' the prophet answered. 'Those who are with us are more than those who are with them.'" Levi Lusko has an incredible retelling of this moment in this story. In an interview with *LifeToday*, Levi says:

> Gehazi looks out the door and sees like a hundred thousand soldiers, and he thinks, "A hundred thousand but more on our side." Okay, so he counts him and Elisha… one… two… and he thinks, "Good thing you got into the ministry because math is clearly not your strong suit, guy." You know he starts feeling bad for the bald-headed prophet to his side, you know, so then Elisha goes, "Oh, you're just looking at it through the naked eye." And then he says, "God help him to see the unseen." Now Gehazi looks again. What does he see? The same soldiers he saw before, they didn't go anywhere. But now, behind them, he sees another army, and what he realized was that the thing that had him surrounded was itself surrounded by God. Now, what's so important about that

is that the Bible doesn't say the angels came when his eyes were opened, but that he could see them. So, they were always there.[1] Second Kings 6:17 says, "And Elisha prayed, 'Open his eyes, Lord, so that he may see.' Then the Lord opened the servant's eyes, and he looked and saw the hills full of horses and chariots of fire all around Elisha."

I believe with all of my heart that God wants nothing more than for us to experience His goodness, His greatness, and His fullness here on earth. I believe God hates our sin, everyone else's sin, and all the pain in the world more than we can even fathom. I believe it breaks His heart far more than it does ours to see us hurting as badly as we do here on earth. I believe He went to the most extraordinary lengths He could have possibly gone to make a way for us to experience life as He intended for it to be by sending His Son to create a means of salvation for us. I believe that through Jesus' life, death, and resurrection, He has defeated sin and death. I believe Jesus was willing to sacrifice Himself because He knew that without it, we would never truly be able to know God's forgiveness and His love. I believe Jesus is coming again to destroy sin and death and restore all of creation to how He intended for it to exist all along.

If we ask God to open our eyes and ears, then He will give us a clearer understanding of what is happening in and around us. He will help us see things as He does. He will give us a new lens and a new perspective to help us understand the hurt and brokenness in the world around us. Not only that, but He will show us how He can use it for His glory. Remember, God never wastes anything.

---

[1] "Levi Lusko: How Christians View Death." *LIFE Today*, 15 Aug. 2016, www.youtube.com/watch?v=IlH2Xx8LWAk.

TWELVE

Do you believe that God wants only good for you, even in whatever place you find yourself standing at this very moment?

Do you believe He understands your pain, hurt, and loss, and wants to touch and heal even your deepest wounds?

Do you believe He wants to help you take off the clouded glasses that are impeding your vision and give you the ability to see your life and your situation the way that He does?

Do you believe He wants to show you and tell you great and unsearchable things when you call on Him?

He does. He wants to bless you. That blessing can come in many forms, but I can assure you that the sweetest form is through an intimate, vulnerable, whole-hearted surrender to a God who replaces chaos with peace and hurt with healing. There is no greater blessing than knowing that He sees and knows exactly what you need long before you even know you need it. But if we just call out to Him and ask Him, then He helps us see and understand how He could be good even on our darkest day.

So often we want to point fingers and ask God where He was on those hard days, when He wants just tell us He was there all along. Just as Gehazi saw in 2 Kings 6, God was already there. He did not show up at the very moment that Gehazi could see what was taking place. He had been there all along.

Sometimes, we believe we have to fight this battle we call life on our own. It is as if we are afraid to bother God with our problems that we do not consider worthy of His time. We place this weight on our shoulders so that we can do it on our own. I can only imagine the pain in God's own heart of watching us try to carry this weight on our own.

I often see that in my son. When he was younger (and even still some today), he worked hard to establish his independence. That usually came in the form of frustration for both of us. He desperately wanted to be able to do everything himself, but he just could not yet.

For example, I recall when he wanted to learn how to tie his shoes. He had cleats and one pair of hiking boots that had laces. So, tying his shoes was not a regular practice for him. But when he was putting either of those shoes on, he took no less than ten minutes attempting to get them tied. Typically, by the time he went to put his shoes on, we were planning to leave in the next five minutes or so. I sat there doing all I could to support him, but also realizing we had somewhere we needed to be. He sat there growing increasingly frustrated as he struggled to tie his shoes.

I eventually broke down and would ask him, "Honey, can I please help you?" And he typically replied with, "No, I can do it!" We sat there a little longer before he finally said, "Mom, I can't do it! Will you please help me?!" I, of course, would rise to the occasion and try to get us both out the door as quickly as humanly possible.

How often are we that elementary-aged child demanding we do things on our own when our loving Father is right there, more than ready and willing to help us if we would just let Him? Indeed, there are times God has equipped us and given us all we need to complete the task before us, but there are also plenty of times we still need Him just as much as we needed help tying our shoes when we were in elementary school. But we have such a hard time letting Him into our secret places to help us.

It is time for us to start realizing, like Elisha did, that a great deal is at stake in our days. There is a war raging around us. We are never fighting

TWELVE

it alone. If we truly realized that, then we would not wear ourselves out and be so exasperated at the end from trying to do it ourselves. God is already at war for us.

Can we trust Him enough to lay down our strength and our abilities at His feet and know that He has it? We must stop letting the fear of man, failure, or whatever else it may be, lead us to believe that we can rely solely on our strength. We need God, like we *really* need God. All we have to do is call on Him, and He is there.

What I knew to be true long before my trip to the mountains, but which God reiterated to me time and again while I was away, is that God's Word is life. I had to stop letting other voices fill my mind. I had to stop valuing other people's opinions as much as I valued His. I had to stop fearing man more than I feared God. I had to stop listening to lies and instead listen to the truth. That is where this song fits in. This song has been my prayer before my quality time with the Lord for quite some time now. I want to let Him guide my understanding of Scripture. I want Him to direct my steps. I do not want to miss Him. Take a moment to pause and listen to the words of "I'm Listening" by Chris McClarney.

I pray wherever you find yourself today that you find hope in these truths of the unchanging character of God.

- *You may feel overcome by fear or feel completely alone, but you can rest in the One who is faithful to keep His promises.*
- *Even though you may feel as if you are being slain, God is on your side, and He is all you need.*
- *The goodness of God is all around you and running hard after you.*

"I'M LISTENING"

- *God is a firm foundation on which you can stand; you are safe with Him.*
- *As hard as it may be to quiet the noise surrounding you, listen for the Lord and look for Him. God is at work.*

God sees you. God hears you. God loves you.

Chapter 6

"Brokenness Aside"

Romans 5:8 says, "But God demonstrates his own love for us in this: While we were still sinners, Christ died for us."

    I debated including the following two chapters. There is no possible way to exclude them and tell you the whole story, but there is also no way to include them without performing open-heart surgery on myself in the pages of this book for all to read. As I write this, I pray fervently for the Lord to give me the words and the strength, while also trusting that if it encourages even one person to see His incomparable love for them and the value He places in creating them, then let it be so.

    My story is intertwined with many others who may not want their story to be shared quite so openly. But there are parts of my story that need to be shared for you to fully understand where I am coming from. Please know that I share this in no way, shape, or form as a condemnation of anyone else for their past sins. As you will soon see, I am fully aware

TWELVE

that I am no better than anyone else. My sins put Jesus on the cross just as much as anyone else's sins did.

Let's start by looking at David, a man after God's own heart. In 2 Samuel 11, David made a choice. Many people jump right to his choice with Bathsheba, but that is not the first choice he made that day. It starts with 2 Samuel 11:1, which says, "In the spring, at the time when kings go off to war, David sent Joab out with the king's men and the whole Israelite army. They destroyed the Ammonites and besieged Rabbah. But David remained in Jerusalem."

The context of this passage sometimes makes it hard for us to discern what was transpiring in that moment. In today's world, very rarely does the leader of the nation go to war. Whether President, Prime Minister, King, or Queen, today the governing authorities of nations work alongside their respective military forces, but they do not engage in direct combat with them. They most certainly are not on the front lines, leading them into battle.

But in the time of David, the king was expected to do precisely that; moreover, he would have been honored to do so. The king would have been the one leading the nation into battle. David should have been the one leading them into battle. But he made a choice. That choice was not to go where he knew he should have been.

Now, what follows in verses 2-5 is something we are more than familiar with when we think of David. Second Samuel 11:2-5 says:

> One evening David got up from his bed and walked around on the roof of the palace. From the roof he saw a woman bathing. The woman was very beautiful, and David sent someone to find out

"BROKENNESS ASIDE"

about her. The man said, "She is Bathsheba, the daughter of Eliam and the wife of Uriah the Hittite." Then David sent messengers to get her. She came to him, and he slept with her. (Now she was purifying herself from her monthly uncleanness.) Then she went back home. The woman conceived and sent word to David, saying, "I am pregnant."

I want to approach this passage of Scripture with great sensitivity, as we all need to do. In case you are not familiar with the terms "exegesis" and "eisegesis," I want to pause and give some background here on how to study Scripture appropriately.

"Exegesis" is the study of what the biblical text says. One of my favorite classes I ever took in college was Exegesis. It was not my favorite class because it was easy; quite frankly, it was probably the most difficult Bible class I took. But I took it with a professor I could not have respected more. He was very careful to teach us to approach Scripture with humility and a recognition that we are not God. We need to understand that there are stories within Scripture where an abundance of detail is shared, and then there are stories where less detail is shared than we would like to have shared. In the abundance or the lack of detail, it is all under God's provision and direct inspiration so that we would be able to see and understand what He desires for us to glean from the story.

This story is one of those stories. There is just enough detail shared that we can take away many facts of the events that transpired. We know David chose to be in the wrong place, leading him to be in a place of immense temptation, and then he decided to dive headfirst into a sinful

TWELVE

situation that was going to have ripple effects on many people. James 1:13-15 says:

> When tempted, no one should say, "God is tempting me." For God cannot be tempted by evil, nor does he tempt anyone; but each person is tempted when they are dragged away by their own evil desire and enticed. Then, after desire has conceived, it gives birth to sin; and sin, when it is full-grown, gives birth to death.

Just as James lays out, death is the result of sin.

Here is where we come back to eisegesis. "Eisegesis" is adding in additional detail or ideas to a passage not otherwise stated. The events between David and Bathsheba throughout the years have had further information added to either pile on David or shift the blame to Bathsheba. I want us to be very careful here, simply taking the details the text shares and seeing what the Lord would have us take away from this story.

What we know to be true is that David saw Bathsheba bathing, he sent someone to bring her to him, she came to him, he slept with her, and she became pregnant. As you continue to read on in 2 Samuel 11, you learn as well that David had her husband placed at the very front of the army, where he died in battle, and then he had Bathsheba brought to his home to be his wife. There is nothing pretty about that story. Nothing is God-glorifying about that story. If you are unfamiliar with the storyline of Scripture, you are probably wondering why David is referred to as a man after God's own heart in Acts 13:22, and rightly so at this point in the story.

Second Samuel 12 follows with Nathan confronting David about his sin. Nathan was a prophet of God. Nathan, through a parable, shares a story with David about a selfish rich man, to which David responds with outrage that someone could seek to serve only themselves. David and Nathan have an honest exchange that opens David's eyes to see just how much destruction he has caused through his choices and the results of those choices, which will impact his entire family, including the child he conceived with Bathsheba. God makes it abundantly clear to David through Nathan that our sin always has a cost. God will never allow us to continue in sin in contentment. Out of love for us, He wants us to truly understand the severity of the choices we make, so that we may also see Him even more clearly in them.

David had a choice to make after Nathan came to him. He could continue to brush aside anyone and everyone to serve himself, or he could take responsibility for his choices. He could truly turn to the Lord with the humblest of hearts, desiring God to forgive him and restore him. If we are being honest, most of us would be quick to tell Nathan to leave because he does not know what he is talking about. Except that he was a prophet, which meant he had been chosen as a spokesperson on behalf of the Lord to the people of Israel, to remind them to keep their eyes fixed on the Lord. David knew there was no way to pretend like Nathan did not know what he was talking about.

So instead, we have recorded for all time not only the sin David chose to commit, but also the cry of his heart in repentance in response to the realization of what he had done. Psalm 51 says:

Have mercy on me, O God, according to your unfailing love; according to your great compassion blot out my transgressions. Wash away all my iniquity and cleanse me from my sin.

TWELVE

For I know my transgressions, and my sin is always before me. Against you, you only, have I sinned and done what is evil in your sight; so you are right in your verdict and justified when you judge. Surely I was sinful at birth, sinful from the time my mother conceived me. Yet you desired faithfulness even in the womb; you taught me wisdom in that secret place.

Cleanse me with hyssop, and I will be clean; wash me, and I will be whiter than snow. Let me hear joy and gladness; let the bones you have crushed rejoice. Hide your face from my sins and blot out all my iniquity.

Create in me a pure heart, O God, and renew a steadfast spirit within me. Do not cast me from your presence or take your Holy Spirit from me. Restore to me the joy of your salvation and grant me a willing spirit, to sustain me.

Then I will teach transgressors your ways, so that sinners will turn back to you. Deliver me from the guilt of bloodshed, O God, you who are God my Savior, and my tongue will sing of your righteousness. Open my lips, Lord, and my mouth will declare your praise. You do not delight in sacrifice, or I would bring it; you do not take pleasure in burnt offerings. My sacrifice, O God, is a broken spirit; a broken and contrite heart you, God, will not despise.

May it please you to prosper Zion, to build up the walls of Jerusalem. Then you will delight in the sacrifices of the righteous, in burnt offerings offered whole; then bulls will be offered on your altar.

"BROKENNESS ASIDE"

Is there anything more beautiful than that? David displays to us today what it looks like to recognize the gravity of our sin and the hurt and destruction it causes to our relationships with God, others, and ourselves. Then he acknowledges that his only hope in that moment is through dependence on God alone. He truly repents of his sin, meaning he desires nothing more than to completely turn away from the road of self-gratification and turn the very opposite direction towards pursuing the Lord. Through that act of repentance, God restores his soul and removes the burden of guilt and shame from him, which leads David to pure and beautiful worship of our gracious and loving God.

That is a man after God's own heart.

Romans 5:6-8 says:

> You see, at just the right time, when we were still powerless, Christ died for the ungodly. Very rarely will anyone die for a righteous person, though for a good person someone might possibly dare to die. But God demonstrates his own love for us in this: While we were still sinners, Christ died for us.

David understood then, long before God revealed the complete picture of salvation He has to us today through His Son, that the only way God would extend His forgiveness to him was to turn to the Lord in humble repentance. The God of the Old Testament is the same as the God of the New Testament. His salvation has always been and always will be readily available to those who desire to turn away from their sin and turn to Him, recognizing that He alone is capable of washing us clean, restoring our souls, and replacing guilt and shame with joy and gladness.

TWELVE

Why in the world did I just go to great lengths to share the story of David and Bathsheba? Their story has always resonated deeply with me. To be more precise, not so much their story but the story of their son.

My life began in a very similar way to their son's life. The details are not necessary at this particular moment. But what is essential to understand is the impact it had on my life, especially as a child. I was not a child who was planned for or even expected, and the beginning of my life meant a significant disruption in other people's lives.

I carried that weight for a long time as a child. No one spoke those words to me directly, but I carried the burden of feeling like my existence was what caused the pain and frustration in my family. I remember when I learned about the sad reality of abortion, and I also remember wondering why in the world my parents did not abort me. I did not know Jesus yet, so I did not understand why I existed. That is a heavy load for a young child to bear.

I became heavily involved in competitive gymnastics at a young age. That became my outlet, where I poured myself into trying to feel like I was worth something in this world. The problem with that is that gymnastics teaches you to strive for perfection. Every toe, finger, and every other part of your body, no matter what event you are participating in, has a correct placement. Anything less than that is a deduction. I love gymnastics still to this day. I get overly excited about watching competitive gymnastics, whether it is at a local university or the Olympics. But for me, gymnastics was a dangerous trap. It led me down a path of feeling like I had to be perfect to prove I had worth.

"BROKENNESS ASIDE"

That carried over to my academics in school. I pushed myself for academic excellence well beyond what was ever necessary or expected of me. The downfall of that is that in school, you receive rewards for that excellence. In both gymnastics and school, I received accolades for an unhealthy pattern that was forming in my life. I received awards for excelling in gymnastics at such a young age. I received praise in school for my determination to the point that I skipped a grade in elementary school. All seemed like it was going well for me, but inside, I was a broken mess.

By the age of seven, my parents divorced. While walking through a horrific divorce process with them, my oldest brother died unexpectedly in a car crash. He was my best friend. Considering how far apart we were in age, it made no sense for us to be as close as we were, but we had a unique and special bond. He brought so much joy to my life. But then, just like that, he was gone.

At the age of eight, I was utterly lost and broken. Life was dark and hopeless. I got really quiet. I stayed quiet for years. I had a hard time believing life held any reason to continue. But by the grace of God, that is when Jesus stepped in.

When my parents divorced, my mom started working nights. My little sister and I spent most nights with this couple who were like grandparents to us and treated us as if we truly were their grandchildren. God gave Mimi an abundance of grace for me. I was hurting. I was lost. I was angry. But she was patient. She was kind. She was faithful to share Jesus with me in a time when I did not want to believe there was a reason to press on.

TWELVE

But eventually I heard what she was saying. I mean, I truly heard it. I started to see the joy in her life and in the lives of the people at the church we went to all the time. I did not know how I felt about it, but it was undeniably evident. I used to shudder at the thought of someone hugging me. We would walk in, and all these people I did not know would hug me, smile, and say hello. I hated it. But I also loved it. I wanted to see why they could be so happy when life was so overwhelmingly hard.

That is when I started to believe maybe there was a reason I existed. For some reason, I had life. For some reason, God created me. For some reason, God was making Himself known to me. I knew very little then, but I knew I wanted to know this Jesus who brought light and life to dark and hopeless situations. I wanted to know this Jesus who gave meaning to life and purpose to His creation. At eight years old, I laid down my anger, frustration, and hurt at the feet of Jesus and begged Him to help me believe He loved me.

I realize that is not the typical story you hear of a young child coming to know Jesus as their Lord and Savior, but that is the reality of where I was at that point. I wish I could say from that day forward, I lived in the love God had for me. I wish I could say that from that day forward, I lived my life overflowing with the joy of His salvation. But I did not.

That struggle of perfectionism continued. As I continued with competitive gymnastics and excelling in academics, my battle continued to grow right along with it, except now I saw it as what I had to maintain to feel deserving of God's love. That was a whole new level of unrealistic weight I was trying to carry on my own. I felt as if I had to present myself as clean and perfect to be seen as someone who knew and loved Jesus.

Yet all I could see was how imperfect I was. I continually fell short of the bar I had set for myself.

Paul says in 1 Timothy 1:15, "Here is a trustworthy saying that deserves full acceptance: Christ Jesus came into the world to save sinners—of whom I am the worst." I could not fathom claiming that to other people. Surely that is not what God wanted of His children. I thought He would want His people to make Him known by how well they seemed to do in life. Without a doubt, that is what would draw people to want to know Jesus for themselves.

Wrong.

There's a quote I heard in college that has never left my mind. It is typically attributed to Augustine, but someone once said, "The church is not a museum for saints, it is a hospital for sinners." If only teenage Amber had understood that, she would have inflicted a lot less damage upon herself.

I went through high school knowing the truth of the gospel found in Scripture in Ephesians 2:8-9, which says, "For it is by grace you have been saved, through faith—and this is not from yourselves, it is the gift of God—not by works, so that no one can boast." I even worked at a church camp for two summers, proclaiming that message to children continually. But I lived as if I had to do everything in my power to be worthy of really receiving the gift of grace.

From the outside, I did that well. I graduated with a perfect GPA. I was Student Council President. I was the football homecoming queen. I was selected as "Best Personality" for the yearbook superlatives. I had

TWELVE

every ambition of becoming a pediatrician and succeeding in all areas of life post-high school.

But something happened in college. Something started to change in me. I realized very quickly in college that I was not invincible. I tried to be. I took anywhere from sixteen to twenty-one hours of classes a semester, which is not an exaggeration. I also worked a minimum of twenty hours per week, but if possible, I would work thirty to forty hours a week across multiple on-campus positions. I was also involved in just about everything one could do while in school. I was in a social club. I directed most of the major events at our university. I was a part of our cheer team. I was involved in numerous committees and served in various roles on campus. I led Bible studies and participated in others. I interned for a children's ministry and a college ministry. I was involved in missions. I was a ringleader in organizing students to attend a worship night each Tuesday at another university. You name it, and I was doing it. Some of it was motivated by a love for the Lord and a deep desire to pursue Him, but a lot of it was me trying to hold it all together.

Until I could no longer hold it together because I got a call that turned my world upside down. The details of that call are not appropriate for me to share in the context of this book. But I lost the battle that had been at war in my mind since I was a child on that day, at least for a time. For the first time, the weight was no longer just from me. Someone else voiced the exact fear I had been trying to fight against my entire life. The girl who was trying to present herself as worthy to God had fully realized that she was, in fact, not worthy. She did not deserve life. She did not deserve love from anyone, but especially not from a perfect God.

"BROKENNESS ASIDE"

As heartbreaking and earth-shattering as that call was, in the absolute best way, the Lord used it to break me of my lifelong struggle with perfectionism. He finally brought me to a place where I was open with Him, and I knew I needed Him more than anything in this world. Without realizing it, I had been utterly terrified that God's grace and mercy just may not be enough to cover all of my brokenness. Hebrews 4:14-16 became more real to me than it ever had before in that moment, which says:

> Therefore, since we have a great high priest who has ascended into heaven, Jesus the Son of God, let us hold firmly to the faith we profess. For we do not have a high priest who is unable to empathize with our weaknesses, but we have one who has been tempted in every way, just as we are—yet he did not sin. Let us then approach God's throne of grace with confidence, so that we may receive mercy and find grace to help us in our time of need.

I found myself reliving this experience one night in Montana, on a quiet and peaceful evening spent reading His Word. It was all I could do to hold it together as I read that passage and spent time singing "Brokenness Aside" to the Lord. If there is one thing I am not afraid to admit now, it is that I need Jesus as much, if not more, than everyone else around me. But I also know beyond a shadow of a doubt that His grace will not run out. Our sin is never too great for Him.

I pray that if you are carrying that weight on your shoulders, you would surrender it to Him. There is nothing you have ever done or ever will do that is too great to be forgiven. Your sins cannot be greater than the price Jesus paid on the cross. Jesus did not just pay for part of your sin or only certain sins through the sacrifice He made. Jesus paid the price for

TWELVE

all of the sins of all people for all of time, and He has extended that forgiveness to every one of us as a gift if we will just receive it. With complete and total joy, God takes our brokenness and makes it beautiful. Take a moment to pause and listen to the words of "Brokenness Aside" by All Sons and Daughters.

I pray wherever you find yourself today that you find hope in these truths of the unchanging character of God.

- *You may feel overcome by fear or feel completely alone, but you can rest in the One who is faithful to keep His promises.*
- *Even though you may feel as if you are being slain, God is on your side, and He is all you need.*
- *The goodness of God is all around you and running hard after you.*
- *God is a firm foundation on which you can stand; you are safe with Him.*
- *As hard as it may be to quiet the noise surrounding you, listen for the Lord and look for Him. God is at work.*
- *God has taken your brokenness and made it beautiful. He redeems our lives and our story.*

God sees you. God hears you. God loves you.

Chapter 7

"Perfectly Loved"

2 Corinthians 5:17 says, "Therefore, if anyone is in Christ, the new creation has come: The old has gone, the new is here!"

There I sat at Sprague Creek Campground in Glacier National Park, roughly 1,600 miles away from where I live, which happens to be the same city where I attended college, being transported back to my nineteen-year-old self as I spent time studying Hebrews 4 on that particular evening. You know, it is funny; I spent years working through the release of perfectionism and the struggle with identity that I battled for the first twenty years of my life. I honestly thought I had overcome the struggle of feeling as though I did not have to be enough for God because Jesus was enough, and He was standing in my place as my substitute. But something happened in 2022 that brought me right back to that place. Divorce has a way of doing that.

TWELVE

In the spring of 2022, I found myself, all of a sudden, feeling like I was not enough all over again. I felt as if I would never be enough for anyone, let alone God. Every lie that had been said to me felt as if it might not be a lie after all. I just wanted to run and hide as far as I could from everyone. But I could not. I had nowhere to run and nowhere to hide. I had to keep putting one foot in front of the other, walking through a storm that I was certain was going to overtake me.

Matthew 8:23-27 felt so very real to me in that particular season. In Matthew 8, Jesus had been ministering to the masses. Crowds of people had been seeking Him, knowing full well He was the One capable of healing them. By the time you get to Matthew 8:23-24, you see just how long a day it had been. Jesus and His disciples got into a boat, and Jesus fell fast asleep. But a massive storm surrounded their boat, which had convinced Jesus' disciples that they were going to drown.

Remember that many of Jesus' disciples were fishermen. They were not unfamiliar with storms at sea. A few years ago, we went on a boat tour in Hawaii. The wake of another boat passing by us made me hold on for dear life to the rail beside me, out of fear that we just might tip over. I had a death grip on my son at all times as he wanted to look out over the edge of the boat at the ocean water down below. I am unfamiliar with being out on the water. I can only imagine the fear that would have set in if the smallest of storms had come along that day. But here were the disciples who were very familiar with life on the water, and yet they were so scared of this storm that they convinced themselves that they were going to drown.

"PERFECTLY LOVED"

The disciples woke up Jesus, begging Him to save them. Jesus replied to them by saying in Matthew 8:26, "'You of little faith, why are you so afraid?' Then he got up and rebuked the winds and the waves, and it was completely calm." Just like that, the storm ceased. For the first time, it seems that these men, who had walked the closest with Jesus during His earthly ministry, finally began to grasp fully what He was capable of accomplishing because He was not just a man. He truly was God.

In the spring of 2022, I knew the storm I was walking into was too much for me to handle on my own. Remember back to the Sunday morning when we sang "Firm Foundation" during worship? That place is where I felt stuck in April of 2022. I saw just how broken and sinful a person I was and still am today. At thirty-four years old, the Lord had continued to do a great work in my life to grow me to be more like Him, but I was nowhere near perfect. I will never be anywhere near perfect on this side of heaven. Being a follower of Christ does not make you sinless; it simply means that as you continue to seek after the Lord, He helps you to sin less.

But in April of 2022, I was overcome with anger. I let the personal hurt I was walking through in a few different areas of life make me hard and angry. That was a decision I made. I knew I was making it too. I could not bring myself to extend forgiveness where I knew I needed to forgive. A *tiny* part of me wanted to extend forgiveness, but I also wanted to remain angry at what was transpiring.

There is most certainly a place for righteous anger. I do not think all anger is sin. In Mark 3, Jesus was in a synagogue on the Sabbath. The Sabbath was a day of rest established in the Old Testament, dating back to the days of creation when God rested on the seventh day. By the time

TWELVE

you get to the New Testament, though, you see that many Jews had misunderstood the purpose of the Sabbath. They had forgotten that God created the Sabbath for them to rest in Him. He did not create them for the Sabbath. On this particular day in Mark 3, a man with an injured hand was present, and onlookers were just waiting for Jesus to do something wrong to accuse Him. In their minds, this included extending mercy to this man and healing his hand.

In Mark 3:4-5, Jesus said:

Then Jesus asked them, "Which is lawful on the Sabbath: to do good or to do evil, to save life or to kill?" But they remained silent. He looked around at them in anger and, deeply distressed at their stubborn hearts, said to the man, "Stretch out your hand." He stretched it out, and his hand was completely restored.

Jesus was angry with these onlookers, knowing the condition of their hearts. In this situation, we see just one of many stories in the Bible where there is a time and a place for anger to exist. It can even be something that reflects God's view of and response to sin.

The difference is in emotion versus action. GotQuestions.org offers a clear explanation of the distinction between these two. The article says:

We all feel emotion... Such feelings come naturally and are not sinful in and of themselves. It is how we act on those emotions that can be sinful. Emotion is internal and not directed against people.

"PERFECTLY LOVED"

Action is external and can be directed positively or negatively toward others.[2]

Ephesians 4:31-32 says, "Get rid of all bitterness, rage and anger, brawling and slander, along with every form of malice. Be kind and compassionate to one another, forgiving each other, just as in Christ God forgave you." That was just it, though. I wanted to be angry. I did not want to extend forgiveness. I remember the words coming out of my mouth, "I know I need to forgive you, but I just do not want to." It was one thing for me to feel the emotion of anger in that moment. I had every justifiable reason to be angry. But I had no reason whatsoever to withhold forgiveness. Mark 11:25 says, "And when you stand praying, if you hold anything against anyone, forgive them, so that your Father in heaven may forgive you your sins." I was building a wall between me and God by misunderstanding how, even in that moment, my response was as sinful as the actions committed by the person who hurt me.

Lysa TerKeurst wrote a book called *Forgiving What You Can't Forget*.[3] God used that book in such a powerful way in my life in that season. In that book, Lysa says many things that I have had to revisit more than once. Here are a few of those quotes:

- "Staying here, blaming them, and forever defining your life by what they did will only increase the pain. Worse, it will keep projecting onto others. The more our pain consumes us, the more it will

---

[2] "In Your Anger Do Not Sin." *GotQuestions.Org*, 10 Jan. 2019, www.gotquestions.org/in-your-anger-do-not-sin.html.

[3] TerKeurst, Lysa. *Forgiving What You Can't Forget*. Nelson Books, 2020.

TWELVE

control us. And sadly, it's those who least deserve to be hurt who our unresolved pain will hurt the most."

- "You can't fake yourself into being okay with what happened. But you can decide that the one who hurt you doesn't get to decide what you do with your memories. Your life can be a graceful combination of beautiful and painful."
- "You're giving yourself too much credit, the only reason you have any grace (to give or receive) is through Christ."

In that particular season of life, I was training for a half-marathon, which might have been the greatest gift of a coping mechanism in that moment. Running is renewing, not only physically but mentally. One night, I went out for a run and just wrestled through this with God. I knew I needed to extend forgiveness. I knew I did not want to extend forgiveness. But I also knew David's prayer from Psalm 51:4, "Against you, you only, have I sinned and done what is evil in your sight; so you are right in your verdict and justified when you judge." I begged God to help me remember the forgiveness He had extended to me because He is a God who is gracious, compassionate, and so very kind. I pleaded with Him to help me believe the words Lysa shared — that I had nothing to offer; I was simply being allowed to be a vessel of God's grace in that moment.

I finally reached a point where I could honestly say, "I forgive you." I had to process and figure out what forgiveness meant in that time and in that relationship. Forgiveness does not always mean complete access to your life again. Forgiveness does not always come with complete reconciliation of relationships here on earth. At times, it certainly can include those things, and at other times, it may not. God has given us hard but beautiful examples of boundaries in Scripture, even in the presence of forgiveness.[4]

All of that came with God opening my eyes to my sin and brokenness. I was hurting immensely. I was dwindling as a person physically because that coping mechanism of running became an unhealthy addiction. Food made me sick. It was not that I wanted to withhold food from myself; I just could not bring myself to eat. I would spend at least two hours and sometimes up to four hours running and walking. I have already shared the battle I was enduring with sleep. All in all, it was just not good.

I did not quite realize it at the time, but in April and May 2022, I found myself back in a place where I was trying to control my circumstances and my feelings to feel worthy of love. Lies rooted in self-control consumed my thoughts. If I were in a little better shape and looked a certain way, my marriage would have been better. If I pushed myself just a little bit farther than I did the last time, I would be just a little bit stronger and able to cope with life's pains a little more next time. If I had been more disciplined in life, I would have been able to hold my family together.

Yes, yes, I know how ridiculous that all sounds now. And the Lord again, in His grace, would make me surrender that to Him. The Wednesday before Thanksgiving in 2022, I had walked and run so very much that I ended up injuring myself. I was out on a run, and this excruciating pain in my knee hit like a freight train. I would then soon find out that the injury I

---

[4] For more on this, see TerKeurst, Lysa. *Good Boundaries and Goodbyes*. Thomas Nelson, 2022.

TWELVE

had brought upon myself was from overuse, and there was nothing I could do to repair it. I had to rest.

I did not want to rest. I wanted to move. I had to move. I had to keep running. I had to keep pressing on. But the Lord simply said, "No. You have to sit down with Me. You need to rest in My arms."

Then came December 2022, when the Lord started to help me see how much I truly needed to just rest in Him. I was annoyed and aggravated at the time, but I knew He was right. There I sat in that room, proctoring a final and wrestling with God about how long He would make me rest in Him before I could run again. I am sure that at that moment, He was just laughing at my stubbornness. Little did I know that He was going to take me on a journey focused on rest, moving forward.

In July 2023, I found myself pondering Hebrews 4:16 in Glacier National Park, which says, "Let us then approach God's throne of grace with confidence, so that we may receive mercy and find grace to help us in our time of need." At that point, I was still not able to run. I had started training my body to be able to hike, but any time I tried to run, it hurt my knee so very badly. That night, my knee was aching from the hikes I had already completed up to that point. I found myself frustrated that I was hurting when I just wanted to be able to go and see all of God's beautiful creation. I was tired of being restricted physically. But the Lord slowed me down that night and helped me see that His mercy and grace were what I needed in my time of need, not to be able to move.

I finally said it all to God. I came to His throne with confidence that He would meet me in it. I told Him I was frustrated. I told Him I was so tired of people in my life, whom I should have been able to trust and rely on, failing me. I was tired of feeling in many ways like I was too much for people and, somehow, in many other ways like I was not enough for people. I was tired of feeling like I was undeserving of being loved wholly. I was tired of believing that everyone who got near me at some point would walk away.

I allowed the opinions of others to fill my mind with the same lies that I had believed from my childhood in those months of my marriage falling apart. Some of them were said with the exact words verbatim as what they had been before. It was like the enemy knew exactly what to say to tear me apart again. Suddenly, adult Amber was back in the same spot as teenage Amber.

This time was different, though, in the fact that this time I was tired of letting lies fill my mind. I knew they were lies. I had prepared myself to wage the war in my mind this time. This time, I picked up my shield and my sword, and I fought back against every lie that filled my mind. As Paul wrote in 2 Corinthians 10:5, "We demolish arguments and every pretension that sets itself up against the knowledge of God, and we take captive every thought to make it obedient to Christ." That is precisely what I did that night. I sat there, reminding myself of who I am in Christ and of truly what His love looks like in my life. I was not giving the enemy an inch of space in my mind. I flooded my mind with truths from His Word. I still have to remind myself of these truths to this day.

- Romans 5:5 says, "And hope does not put us to shame, because God's love has been poured out into our hearts through the Holy Spirit, who has been given to us."
- Romans 8:1 says, "Therefore, there is now no condemnation for those who are in Christ Jesus."

TWELVE

- Lamentations 3:22-24 says, "Because of the Lord's great love we are not consumed, for his compassions never fail. They are new every morning; great is your faithfulness. I say to myself, 'The Lord is my portion; therefore I will wait for him.'"
- Second Corinthians 5:17 says, "Therefore, if anyone is in Christ, the new creation has come: The old has gone, the new is here!"
- Galatians 2:20 says, "I have been crucified with Christ and I no longer live, but Christ lives in me. The life I now live in the body, I live by faith in the Son of God, who loved me and gave himself for me."
- First John 3:1 says, "See what great love the Father has lavished on us, that we should be called children of God! And that is what we are! The reason the world does not know us is that it did not know him."
- First John 4:10 says, "This is love: not that we loved God, but that he loved us and sent his Son as an atoning sacrifice for our sins."

That night, the Lord reminded me that He completely and perfectly loved me. I had been made new by the blood of the Lamb. I once had been overcome by sin, but I had been set free by the One who overcame sin Himself. The lies no longer held authority in my life. I did not have to wear that identity. Instead, I could put on the truth of who I am in Christ.

- I am chosen and dearly loved. I am God's special possession (1 Peter 2:9).
- I am a new creation. My old self is no more (2 Corinthians 5:17).
- My body is a temple of the Holy Spirit. God's Spirit is within me (1 Corinthians 3:16).

- I am a part of the body of Christ. I have a place where I belong among the family of God (Ephesians 2:19-22).
- I am Christ's ambassador. God is going to make Himself known through me (2 Corinthians 5:20).
- I am a light in a dark world. As God works in my life, He will shine through me so that others may be drawn to Him (Matthew 5:14-16).
- Apart from Christ, I can do nothing. But with Him there will be growth and fruit and life in my life (John 15:4-5).

That evening, God reminded me that He never asks me to be enough to be worthy of being used by Him. He never asks that of you either. Instead, He reminds us continually in Scripture that it is simply a recognition that we are not enough on our own that opens the door for Him to do great and mighty things in and through us. We have to take our eyes off ourselves. If we continue to look at ourselves, expecting to find a good enough reason for God to choose to use us, then we will attempt to draw people after ourselves rather than pointing them to God. We will also be continually let down because we will be searching for a reason to deem ourselves worthy every day of our lives. Nothing good comes from that. But when we recognize that the only good within us is the work of the Lord, then we are more compelled to share with people that He alone is worth pursuing after. He is who we point people towards.

I recognize that many people reading this may not have endured the circumstances I have in life that led to an internal battle of worth. Yet, I have sat with enough people of all ages to be able to say with absolute certainty that this is a battle we all face to some extent. I find it interesting

TWELVE

that the premise of the message of salvation is that we cannot save ourselves (hence the reason Jesus came), and yet we struggle with really believing God could look at us with our sin and say, "I love you. I forgive you. You are mine." The enemy is good at his job. He is a great deceiver.

The question then is, will you continue to feel as if you need to clean yourself up to come before the Lord, or recognize that He is the one who makes you clean?

Will you let Him take the broken areas of your life and make them your testimony of how He has worked to transform you from the inside out?

Will you stop running and hiding from whatever that may be for you (sin, person, circumstance, experience, thought, etc.) and believe that God is there and ready to catch you if you would just fall into His arms?

Will you surrender what you thought your life should have looked like and trust that He can take what is and use it for His glory?

That one hits too close to home for me. That is the place I have been in for quite some time now, where I almost daily have to pray for the Lord to give me the strength to believe. I find myself wanting to just go through life keeping my head down and curling back up into my shell, like the quiet girl I was roaming the halls of my elementary school, middle school, junior high, and high school. Yet the Lord keeps reminding me He has a beautiful story to bring to life in this season.

Romans 8:28 says, "And we know that in all things God works for the good of those who love him, who have been called according to his purpose." God can and will use all things for His glory and our good. Even with what may have initially been out of disobedience and outright rebellion against Him, He can flip the script and make even *that* be the testimony of His great work in your life.

If you are in a place where you struggle to believe the Lord loves you, let the words of this song reverberate to the depths of your soul, the very words the Lord speaks over you. You are dearly loved. Take a moment to pause and listen to the words of "Perfectly Loved" by Rachael Lampa.

I pray wherever you find yourself today that you find hope in these truths of the unchanging character of God.

- *You may feel overcome by fear or feel completely alone, but you can rest in the One who is faithful to keep His promises.*
- *Even though you may feel as if you are being slain, God is on your side, and He is all you need.*
- *The goodness of God is all around you and running hard after you.*
- *God is a firm foundation on which you can stand; you are safe with Him.*
- *As hard as it may be to quiet the noise surrounding you, listen for the Lord and look for Him. God is at work.*
- *God has taken your brokenness and made it beautiful. He redeems our lives and our story.*
- *Rather than looking upon you with shame, God looks upon you with perfect love.*

God sees you. God hears you. God loves you.

Chapter 8

"Just as Good"

Nahum 1:7 says, "The Lord is good, a refuge in times of trouble. He cares for those who trust in him."

Within the church, we often do ourselves a disservice by believing that our testimony is a one-and-done event that results in our justification, which is the moment of salvation when God exchanges our sin for Christ's forgiveness. We often forget that our lives are a continual testimony of the Lord teaching, growing, and molding us into the person He desires us to be. We are on a lifelong journey of being sanctified, which is the process of becoming more and more like Christ every day, that we will never complete here in this lifetime. It will be brought to completion in Heaven through glorification, the moment that God completely eradicates the presence of sin.

The Lord has used the last several years of my life as a greater testimony of His work in my heart and life. But I also know that He is still

TWELVE

teaching me. He is still growing me. He is still molding me. But I want to be here for it. I want to be open to all He still has ahead for me.

Hebrews 4 reminds us that Jesus understands our struggle with temptation because He was tested in every way here on earth that we will face even today. As He endured the suffering this broken world threw His way, and continues to throw at us today, He modeled for us perfect obedience. However, He did not model perfect obedience in a way that expected us to follow in His steps. That suffering He endured that He was obedient through made a way for Him to be our perfect, spotless lamb sacrificed for the atonement (or the forgiveness) of our sins. The existence of sin in our lives is the very reason we cannot pay for our sins. Choosing to sin blemishes us. But Christ, being perfect in obedience, was an acceptable sacrifice for all sin for all people for all of time. He accomplished what we never could. Only He is capable of saving us. Only He is deserving of worship. Only He is worthy of pursuing with all of our hearts.

Hebrews 4:14-16 holds beautiful truths. These truth-bearing verses then follow in Hebrews 5:7-10, which says:

> During the days of Jesus' life on earth, he offered up prayers and petitions with fervent cries and tears to the one who could save him from death, and he was heard because of his reverent submission. Son though he was, he learned obedience from what he suffered and, once made perfect, he became the source of eternal salvation for all who obey him and was designated by God to be high priest in the order of Melchizedek.

I completed several smaller hikes in Glacier before embarking on the Grinnell Glacier hike in Glacier National Park, which I shared about in the first chapter. I hiked the Trail of the Cedars/Avalanche Lake Trail, Hidden Lake Overlook, and the Three Falls Trail. I ended up walking and hiking just over seventeen miles that day. But I also had a strange occurrence that day with a sweet family from Nebraska.

I started that morning at the Trail of the Cedars/Avalanche Lake Trail, which a friend had highly recommended to me, and it did not disappoint. I had shared with someone the day before that I planned to do those hikes, and I asked what order I should do them in. They told me to start at the Trail of the Cedars/Avalanche Lake Trail because it was closest to my campsite, but also because it had the least amount of parking available. The earlier, the better, to access that trail more easily. That is what I did.

I think that was the best decision overall, but all I know is by the time I got to the Hidden Lake Overlook, the parking lot for that trail was utterly insane. I mentioned before that when I was trying to find parking for the Highline Trail, I drove around for about forty-five minutes. Well, I knew that was coming when I went to find parking that day, because these trails shared a parking lot. On the day I completed the Hidden Lake Overlook, I drove around for almost two hours looking for parking.

As a side note, it would be great if there were a system for the next person in line to park in the next available spot after someone leaves, but that is not how Glacier National Park works. Instead, the system is that cars that have multiple passengers in them have their additional passengers get out and ask people as they are walking towards the parking lot if they can have their spot, and then direct the driver of their car to follow them

TWELVE

to the place the people would soon be pulling out of, so that they can then park there.

That sounds wonderful, except I was there by myself. I had no one to get out and find someone who was exiting the parking lot to reserve a spot for me. So, I drove around the parking lot for a very long time. I was at the point where I was debating bypassing that trail altogether. Had it not been listed as one of the must-see spots of Glacier National Park, I would have just driven on by.

There was a family that looked like they might be leaving, climbing into their van as I passed behind them. I kindly asked them if they were about to leave. They informed me they were not leaving. They were just grabbing their lunches. They commented on the chaos of the parking lot, and I shared with them that I had been driving around it for nearly two hours. We laughed, and I continued driving in circles.

Within a few moments, one of the girls came running up to my car. She said, "Hey, we all like you! We want you to have our parking spot! We were going to stay here and eat, but we all decided we are going to take our lunch to go so that you can have our parking spot!" I was shocked but also *OVERJOYED*! I pulled around to the aisle where they were parked, and sure enough, they waited for me. They barricaded their spot for me so that I could pull into it before someone else did.

I thanked them as much as I possibly could have at that moment. I was finally able to go and enjoy the beautiful hike, which is fully deserving of its reputation as one of the most highly recommended trails in Glacier National Park. Mountain goats and big-horned sheep filled the trail, and the beauty of the never-ending mountain range that makes up Glacier

National Park surrounded the area. It climaxed with an overlook of Hidden Lake (obviously), which fulfills every image you have in your mind of a beautiful, turquoise lake in the mountains. I was so very grateful to have had the opportunity to hike that trail and look out over God's beautiful creation.

After the Hidden Lake Overlook, I went on to the Three Falls. I already told you that at my campsite at Jenny Lake Campground, I greeted every person who came to get water. Well, I did the same while I was out hiking. I was walking somewhere between Baring Falls and St. Mary's Falls when I crossed paths with this family who came from the opposite direction. Naturally, I said hi and asked them how they were before I realized it was that family that had let me have their parking spot!

I quickly thanked them again for letting me park there. We talked about the beauty of the Hidden Lake Overlook. In that conversation, the family shared with me that they could not believe I kept driving around that parking lot and yet still had so much joy, excitement, and a willingness to keep waiting. I laughed and told them I was seriously on the verge of giving up and driving away, but I was glad I did not. Then the dad asked me if I was there alone. I shared with them that I had just taken a trip with Jesus, enjoying His beautiful creation. We had a short but sweet conversation, exchanging all the truly magnificent things we had encountered in our time outdoors over the previous few days. We said farewell, and we went our separate ways.

After I crawled back to my campsite at the end of that day, my legs were so very weary, and my knee was very worn out. I kept thinking about that conversation with that precious family from Nebraska. The days

TWELVE

leading up to this moment, as I mentioned, I walked back through the most complex parts of my life, the darkest thoughts I had wrestled with, and fought against them with the truth of God's Word. I had found myself that day ready to take on the world. I had reminded myself that the God who sought me out at eight years old, who replaced my mourning with dancing, was the same God who sought me out at nineteen years old, who replaced my shame of being imperfect with confidence in the perfect One. He was the same God who sought me out at thirty-four years old, who replaced my weakness and defeat with strength and victory.

I had come to realize that what I had experienced that day was exactly what I would experience moving forward in my life. I was going to go through frustrating experiences that logically made no sense. I was going to endure things that seemed like I should have been able to avoid them so easily. I was going to feel perplexed and annoyed at myself and others for the sin we brought into the world every day of my life. But I was also going to have to figure out how to keep pressing on with joy found only in the Lord and anticipation of what He has in store for the road ahead.

That evening, I reflected on Joshua 4, where the Israelites crossed the Jordan River and created a pile of rocks to remember God's goodness and faithfulness. We have already talked about how God parted the Red Sea for the Israelites to escape from the Egyptian army, but that is not the only time the Lord parted waters for the sake of protecting the Israelites. In Joshua 3:12-13, Joshua said to the Israelites, "Now then, choose twelve men from the tribes of Israel, one from each tribe. And as soon as the priests who carry the ark of the Lord—the Lord of all the earth—set foot in the Jordan, its waters flowing downstream will be cut off and stand up in a heap." The passage even goes on to say that the water was at flood level during this particular season, but everything transpired exactly as the Lord said it would.

In Joshua 4:21-24, Joshua said to the Israelites:

In the future, when your descendants ask their parents, "What do these stones mean?" tell them, "Israel crossed the Jordan on dry ground." For the Lord your God dried up the Jordan before you until you had crossed over. The Lord your God did to the Jordan what he had done to the Red Sea when he dried it up before us until we had crossed over. He did this so that all the peoples of the earth might know that the hand of the Lord is powerful and so that you might always fear the Lord your God.

I am sure some people passed by the stack of rocks without noticing them. But to the people of God, this was more than a random pile of stones. It was a reminder of God's goodness and faithfulness throughout many generations. He was a God who saw them and was with them.

The Old Testament is full of moments where Israel would erect a memorial of some kind, not to be worshiped, but simply as a visible, tangible reminder of God's work among them. First Samuel 7 is another example of this type of event taking place. Samuel was a prophet known for anointing the first two kings of Israel, Saul and David. The transition from judges to kings for Israel was not a smooth one, to say the least. Judges 21:25 says, "In those days Israel had no king; everyone did as they saw fit." Israel was in a place of complete and total idolatry and self-serving

TWELVE

lifestyles. But, by the grace of God, by the time you get to 1 Samuel 7, Israel has truly repented of their idolatry and turned back to the Lord.

As the Israelites gathered together to fast, confess, and repent of their selfishness and pride, the Philistine army had been informed that they were assembled in one place. When it seemed like Israel had their defenses down because they were focused on pursuing their Defender rather than defending themselves, 1 Samuel 7:10 says, "The Philistines drew near to engage Israel in battle." But 1 Samuel 7:10 does not end there. It goes on to say, "But that day the Lord thundered with loud thunder against the Philistines and threw them into such a panic that they were routed before the Israelites."

The Israelites were fully aware that they could only attribute the victory in that battle to the Lord. First Samuel 7:12 says, "Then Samuel took a stone and set it up between Mizpah and Shen. He named it Ebenezer, saying, 'Thus far the Lord has helped us.'" Each time an Israelite would have passed by the stone of Ebenezer, they would have remembered God's protection and His power. God's faithfulness to restore the repentant nation of Israel had been on full display that day.

In Psalm 105:1-2, it says, "Give praise to the Lord, proclaim his name; make known among the nations what he has done. Sing to him, sing praise to him; tell of all his wonderful acts." Many times in the Psalms, we see David and the other authors looking back to remember who God has been in the past, reminding themselves of who He is in their present circumstances as well. This recounting of God's faithfulness would then give them the strength to believe they could endure whatever hardship lay before them in that moment and know that He would remain the same God in the future, no matter what may come.

Stones of remembrance can take the form of people, places, events, among many other things, where God has shown His faithfulness in your life. As I stop and look back over my life, here are some of the monumental stones where I can see God's faithfulness:

- 1995 - The loss of my brother - My brother's passing, which the Lord used to help me see my need for Him
- 1995 - Harvest Time Tabernacle - The church I attended in Fort Smith, Arkansas, where I heard the gospel for the first time and chose to surrender my life to the Lord
- 2003 - Dry Gulch, U.S.A. - The church camp I worked at the summer after my sophomore year of high school, which would change my life in every way moving forward
- 2003-2005 - Lincoln Christian School - The first Christian school I attended, which opened my eyes to a love and passion for Christian education
- 2006 – The Church at Battle Creek - The summer I spent with The Church at Battle Creek, wrestling with how the Lord planned to use my gifts and passions in my life for His glory and His plan, not my own
- 2008 - Mexico mission trip - My first mission trip that cultivated a love for other cultures and provided understanding of the call in the Great Commission to make disciples among all nations

TWELVE

- 2012 - Belgium mission trip - An opportunity the Lord used that created a new passion in ministry that would impact my life more than I ever expected
- 2016 - The birth of my son - The greatest blessing the Lord has ever provided to teach me more about His love for me than anything else ever has or ever will
- 2017 - Oklahoma Christian School - An unexpected opportunity that has created a whole new community in my life, which has been a tremendous blessing to me
- 2022 - Vancouver mission trip - A week I saw the Lord move more visibly and intimately in my life than I ever have, that I will genuinely never forget

Each of these has a more detailed story I could share; some of them I already have.

In moments of difficulty, what we see God commanding the Israelites to do in the Old Testament is to remember who God has always been. We often rush through life, moving on to the next thing without taking time to stop and look back. However, special monuments, festivals, or days where it is clear that it was a regular practice for Israel to remind themselves of who God was in the past as an encouragement to hold tightly to Him in the present fill the pages of the Old Testament. We could benefit from taking a page from their book.

I encourage you to take a moment to reflect on how you have seen God in your life. There may be a specific place where the Lord has taken you to reveal to you more about who He is as the Creator of all things. There may be an experience you had that the Lord walked with you

"JUST AS GOOD"

through to show you how and why He made you exactly as you are to make Him known and bring Him glory. There may be a person the Lord used to help you see and understand God's incomparable and unconditional love for you.

Some of my stones of remembrance were some of the hardest seasons the Lord walked with me through. Many of them were no cake walk. God used them in incredible ways to reveal Himself to me, but they did not come without some bumps, bruises, and scars along the way. Some of your stones of remembrance may not be from a place of all sunshine and rainbows. My list most certainly is not. That is okay. God is the same God on the mountain top as He is in the valley down below.

Nahum 1:7 says, "The Lord is good, a refuge in times of trouble. He cares for those who trust in him." That sounds just peachy when you read that verse. But the context of Nahum is as far from peachy as one could be. Nahum follows the story of Jonah. In the story of Jonah, God had called Jonah to go to the people of Nineveh to call them to repentance. But Jonah did not want the Ninevites to have the opportunity to repent. He went as far away from Nineveh as he possibly could have. Through drastic measures and God's grace, Jonah ultimately goes to Nineveh, proclaiming the message of salvation to the Ninevites, and they repent and turn to the Lord.

Nahum takes place around one hundred and fifty years later in the same place, but at that point, the new generation of people had turned back to evil ways, away from the Lord. Nahum was assigned the same task as Jonah, only this time, the people of Nineveh would not repent. God would rightly judge them for their evil ways. In his call to repentance,

TWELVE

Nahum reminded the Ninevites of Nahum 1:7, "The Lord is good, a refuge in times of trouble. He cares for those who trust in him."

As we navigate our lives, facing trials of all different forms, I pray that we remember that the Lord is good. God truly is our refuge, our safe place in those times of immense difficulty and pain. God loves us fiercely, and He cares about us more deeply than we can even imagine. God is the same God who parted the Red Sea and the Jordan River to lead His people into safety. God is the same God who provides the power and protection we need when facing battles that are too much for us to face on our own. God is the same God who meets repentance with forgiveness, no matter how far our sin seems to have separated us from Him. Romans 15:13 says, "May the God of hope fill you with all joy and peace as you trust in him, so that you may overflow with hope by the power of the Holy Spirit."

In moments where we find ourselves wanting to doubt God's goodness, His willingness to love us, or His ability to cover over the multitude of our sins, I hope the words of this song remind us of His unchanging, abundant goodness. Take a moment to pause and listen to the words of "Just as Good" by Chris Renzema.

I pray wherever you find yourself today that you find hope in these truths of the unchanging character of God.

- *You may feel overcome by fear or feel completely alone, but you can rest in the One who is faithful to keep His promises.*
- *Even though you may feel as if you are being slain, God is on your side, and He is all you need.*
- *The goodness of God is all around you and running hard after you.*

"JUST AS GOOD"

- *God is a firm foundation on which you can stand; you are safe with Him.*
- *As hard as it may be to quiet the noise surrounding you, listen for the Lord and look for Him. God is at work.*
- *God has taken your brokenness and made it beautiful. He redeems our lives and our story.*
- *Rather than looking upon you with shame, God looks upon you with perfect love.*
- *God is just as good today as He was when He first made Himself known to you.*

God sees you. God hears you. God loves you.

Chapter 9

"Highlands"

1 John 4:4 says, "You, dear children, are from God and have overcome them, because the one who is in you is greater than the one who is in the world."

As my perspective shifted regarding the circumstances I found myself in, what I saw God as capable of accomplishing changed right along with it. Hebrews 6:19-20 says:

> We have this hope as an anchor for the soul, firm and secure. It enters the inner sanctuary behind the curtain, where our forerunner, Jesus, has entered on our behalf. He has become a high priest forever, in the order of Melchizedek.

Just a few weeks ago, our school held a chapel specifically on these verses. Before delving into the context of the passage and its application, the speaker talked about an anchor in general. One of the things he discussed was how an anchor has no value to us when we are in shallow or calm

TWELVE

waters. But when we are in the midst of a storm, that anchor becomes our lifeline.

This hope, reiterated in Hebrews, dates back to the beginning of the letter, where the author makes it clear that our hope rests solely in Christ. He is firm and secure. He is unchanging. He is the reason we have an unshakable hope that withstands any storm. He is interceding on our behalf. He is standing in our place. He will continue to fight for us all the days of our lives.

It is easy to stand in the shallows and say that we will have unwavering faith in God, but sometimes God calls us to the deeps, where we have to depend on Him entirely. We do not tend to prefer that place, and yet it is the best place to be as long as we anchor ourselves to the One who is firm and secure. We often get worried when the storm comes, wondering if our anchor can hold us steady, while God knows that nothing can break us when we have Him on our side.

When God calls us to the deep, what are we going to do? When we find ourselves in the valley of the shadow of death, how are we going to respond? When the story of our lives takes an unexpected turn, what are we going to do with it?

I did not fully understand how two conflicting emotions could coexist simultaneously until 2022. Up to that point, I always thought of my life as being either at the highest possible peak of a mountain top or at the base of the deepest of valleys. I often defined the emotions of life as a place along a spectrum between joy and sadness. I did not realize that is how I viewed life, but it was indeed how I was categorizing things, whether I was aware of it or not.

"HIGHLANDS"

It was not until the summer of 2022 that I found myself trying to understand how I could have grief and joy in concert with one another. I began to realize that it is the mountain top and the valley together that bring a deep appreciation for each one individually. I was walking through the grief of accepting what had transpired and where the road was leading, while also experiencing joy in knowing that God was walking with me all along the way. It seemed like those two things could not work together, yet they were working in beautiful unison to help me process through where I was in that given moment. I was both in the valley and on the mountain top.

I had come to believe that if I still had breath in my lungs, then God still had a plan for my life. I knew full well that God did not make mistakes. My life was not a mistake. The place I found myself standing in was not a mistake. God could and would use every single bit of it if I let Him. I most certainly did not understand how, in that moment, He would use any ounce of what I had walked through for His glory, but He knew.

When we lost our referral, we tried to explain to our precious five-year-old why his brother, whom he had longed for and prayed for, would no longer be coming home to us. That was one of many hard conversations we had with him during that season. But rather than respond in anger, frustration, or bitterness, he responded with empathy and concern. He wanted to know if his little brother was going to be okay. He wanted to know if his brother would ever have a family. He wanted to know if his brother would ever understand what it was like to be loved and cared for, just as we had prayed he would experience in our home.

TWELVE

It took all I had in me every time we had that conversation to refrain from breaking down, because the truth was that I had those same questions. But I reiterated to him and myself time and time again, "God loves him even more than we do. He will take care of him." Every time I said that, my son responded with the same question, "But how do you know that?"

How did I know that? Did I believe that was true? Was God going to take care of him? Was God going to take care of us?

That was a doozy of a question in those moments that multiplied into many other questions in my mind. The honest answer was that I did not know. I could not fathom how God would take care of each of us early on in that journey. But I kept clinging to that anchor of hope.

Hebrews 11:1 says, "Now faith is confidence in what we hope for and assurance about what we do not see." I could not see even the tiniest glimpse initially of how there could be anything good in this scenario. That was at the peak of my anger and frustration. But as time went on, I kept telling God and my son in those moments, "I really do not know how God is going to answer the prayers we have prayed, but what I do know is that He will. It is going to look different from what we ever thought it would. But I know He will."

We had been very public about our adoption; hundreds (quite literally hundreds) of people had partnered with us in prayer and in making it possible financially for us to adopt this little boy. I will forever be grateful for the community of people near and far who rallied with us in the process of opening the door of opportunity for us to adopt. God moved hearts to give abundantly through donating some of their services, giving financially, eating at local restaurants, and supporting other organizations that supported our adoption. It was incredible to see God work through so many unexpected means to help us proceed in that journey. Our community was as invested in our adoption as we were.

When we shared that we would not be able to adopt him anymore, it was no longer just our son asking me questions; it was about anyone and everyone asking me questions. I could not, and still cannot, share the details of that publicly, but the sting of doubt grew more and more with each person with the best of intentions reaching out just wanting to understand. I remember the day after we shared on social media that we could no longer bring home that sweet boy. A student, who is more like family to me, walked into my room and, with tears in her eyes, hugged me. She felt the seriousness of the loss herself. She was not the only one. It did not matter whether I was at school, a sporting event, church, Target, or dinner with friends; tears filled the eyes of those around us. There was comfort in knowing that others were feeling the pain alongside us, but frustration was also building within me as I realized that this had been the outcome of the whole process.

How could we come this far and this be the result?

How could God let this happen?

I found myself teetering on the edge of allowing those questions to consume me. I mustered all the strength I possibly could to make it through that season before finally just collapsing into the Lord's arms. But the Lord in His grace caught me and held me.

I was not the first, and I most certainly would not be the last, to be asked to trust a child into the hands of the Lord.

TWELVE

- Abraham and Sarah had to surrender Isaac into the hands of the Lord (Genesis 22:8).
- Amram and Jochebed had to surrender Moses into the hands of the Lord (Exodus 2:3).
- David and Bathsheba had to surrender their son into the hands of the Lord (2 Samuel 12:15-16).
- God Himself surrendered His own Son (John 3:16).

Psalm 34:17-18 says, "The righteous cry out, and the Lord hears them; he delivers them from all their troubles. The Lord is close to the brokenhearted and saves those who are crushed in spirit." That is precisely what happened.

By nothing more than the grace of the Lord, someone shared with me that a family was going to adopt the little boy who would forever remain in our hearts — a family that I had befriended along the adoption journey. They were going to provide him with a home, a family, and unconditional love, but they also would share the hope of Christ with him. If you remember, that had been my prayer all along in the adoption process. Every single thing we had been praying would come to pass for this precious little boy; it would just take place in a different home.

There was a part of me that was ecstatic about being able to give the reason for the hope that I had held so tightly to, even in the unknown, to my son. There was another part of me that was devastated that those things had to take place in a different home. To this day, if you ask my son if he has any siblings, he will tell you that he has a brother whom he loves, but who will never live with him. That is the truth. That little boy will forever be a part of our family and a void in our hearts. But the Lord has been so faithful to hear our prayers for him and remind us that He has him in His hands. He loves him even more than we do. I understood that day more than I ever had what surrender truly meant.

Mark 14:16 says, "'Abba, Father,' he said, 'everything is possible for you. Take this cup from me. Yet not what I will, but what you will.'" Jesus modeled perfect surrender, even when it came at the expense of His own life. Jesus recognized God's limitless power. Jesus trusted that if God was capable of anything, then His will was precisely what needed to take place. Jesus believed that the will of God was always good, even if, in the moment, it may not have appeared that way.

Ephesians 3:20-21 says, "Now to him who is able to do immeasurably more than all we ask or imagine, according to his power that is at work within us, to him be glory in the church and in Christ Jesus throughout all generations, for ever and ever! Amen." Our prayer today, even in the most hopeless of moments, is the same as Jesus' prayer was that night in the Garden of Gethsemane, and as Paul declares to the people of Ephesus.

God, I know You have all power in heaven and on earth. I trust that You are capable of anything. If this is in Your will, give me the ability to hold tightly to Your goodness through it all. May You be glorified in it.

When I was in high school and college, writing poetry became a way for me to pour my heart out to God. I would occasionally write silly poems for friends and share them with them, but I never let anyone else read the genuine, heartfelt poems. I wrote them for me and God alone. No one even knew about them. I am not sure at what point that stopped, but I know I have not taken the time to do that since college. That time

TWELVE

between me and the Lord used to be a truly sacred time with Him. I would drive out to the lake near our college campus by myself and sit there, using whatever journal I had at the time, and write. It was just me and God.

I have lost all of those journals from that season. More than that, I honestly forgot about that time entirely until recently. It was not until just before my trip that I started writing poetry again. Now, I am not a trained poet. It is simply a way for me to connect with God on a deeper, heart-level than typical prayer journaling. Also, please be aware that this is the most vulnerable part of me that I am displaying in this book.

I spent a good portion of my time away in the mountains, processing specifically through the hole in my heart that remained after losing the ability to adopt that little boy. I told you about the conversation I had with a pastor and his wife at a local coffee shop, where we talked through what had been unraveling in my life. They had been there throughout our entire adoption journey. As I talked through how acutely painful the hurt in my heart was over this precious child, he reminded me that I was going to have to grieve this the same as if it were the death of a child, like in a miscarriage. He was right. We had been "paper pregnant" for sixty-two months. Though I had never heard this child's heartbeat or carried his little body within my own body, the loss I felt in losing him was just as painful.

Two days after I got home, I wrote this poem.

"The Boy I'll Never Hold"
I waited for you and I prayed for you
I longed for the day you would be near

"HIGHLANDS"

I told everyone before I even knew who
I could not wait for you to be here

You are the boy I always longed for
A precious soul in the body of a three-year-old
You are the one I knew I would adore
I dreamed of how our lives would unfold
I'll always love you at my deepest core
But you'll always be the boy I'll never hold

After years of being a number on a list
We finally got the call with your name
The emotions that followed, I couldn't resist
My love for you, I could only proclaim

You are the boy I always longed for
A precious soul in the body of a three-year-old
You are the one I knew I would adore
I dreamed of how our lives would unfold
I'll always love you at my deepest core
But you'll always be the boy I'll never hold

I may never understand God's time or plan
He used you in a special way to change me forever
There are no regrets that our journey began
I hope you know I'll deeply love you, however

TWELVE

> You are the boy I always longed for
> A precious soul in the body of a three-year-old
> You are the one I knew I would adore
> I dreamed of how our lives would unfold
> I'll always love you at my deepest core
> But you'll always be the boy I'll never hold

Here is what I came to conclude about this longing of my heart while I was away that summer. No replacement or filler can seal the gap in my heart for that sweet boy. That is an area I still struggle to see and understand how God will fulfill the desires of my heart. But I believe He can. Moreover, I believe He will. I know full well it may never be fulfilled here on earth, but I believe with all of my heart that it will be in Heaven someday. That may be the only way that healing can fully take place in that particular area of my life, but I know there is a day coming when the healing will come to pass. But I also know I cannot spend my life holding onto and longing for what I thought life should have been. I had to come to a place of being willing to loosen my grip from whatever in life I could find to cling to and open my hands to what the Lord may have in store for me.

First John 4:4 says, "You, dear children, are from God and have overcome them, because the one who is in you is greater than the one who is in the world." That passage goes on to say in 1 John 4:18-19, "There is no fear in love. But perfect love drives out fear... We love because he first loved us." First John 4 reminds me that I do not have to fear what is or what will be in my story. I do not have to be defeated by the disappointment that has come my way. Understanding the love God has for me can change my perspective on everything else. God understands loss. God understands pain. God understands disappointment. He gets it all.

I had to decide how I was going to respond to that loss. Was I going to allow it to lead me down a path of doubt and frustration in the Lord and what He allows to take place here on earth, at least for a time? Or was I going to trust in His goodness and His ability to overcome every hard thing I had faced and will continue to face in this life?

That in no way, shape, or form means I have to push out the grief of losing the ability to ever truly know that little boy. I do not have to pretend like my heart is entirely okay with the fact that I will never see him smile or hear him laugh. I do not have to act like it does not break my heart into pieces to know that my son still talks about the brother he wishes he had at home, one he could share all his favorite things and tell his favorite stories. That all hurts. It does not hurt the same as it did a year and a half ago, but it still hurts. To an extent, I am sure it always will.

No, what it means is that I can recognize that grief in my life and in that very moment be able to say, "God, I cannot carry this load on my own. Please help me. Please take this heavy yoke that is too much for me to carry. Help me see and believe that You are the ultimate fulfillment of every desire I have. Help me to long for You more than anything else. Help me to surrender the plans I had for my life and trust my future into Your hands. You have me in Your hands. You have all of us in Your hands. Help me hold to that truth."

TWELVE

In 2 Corinthians 6:8, Paul says that he is "sorrowful, yet always rejoicing." I could see and recognize and acknowledge the grief I was experiencing, while I could also see and recognize and acknowledge the joy I had in Christ, His salvation, and the promise that He is going to come again. Grief and joy can co-exist in a messy but beautiful way. Isaiah 26:8 says, "Yes, Lord, walking in the way of your laws, we wait for you; your name and renown are the desire of our hearts." Colossians 1:15-17 says:

> The Son is the image of the invisible God, the firstborn over all creation. For in him all things were created: things in heaven and on earth, visible and invisible, whether thrones or powers or rulers or authorities; all things have been created through him and for him. He is before all things, and in him all things hold together.

Many of the hours I spent driving from place to place while on the trip were filled with worship sessions and prayers. Sometimes they were also just good old jam sessions and dance parties. But in the moments where they were intimate and deeply personal between me and God, I found myself remembering that He is what I desired more than anything else. I knew He was holding my life together, but I had to speak that over myself. I knew He was working in my heart, but I had to remind myself of that.

Psalm 51:12 says, "Restore to me the joy of your salvation and grant me a willing spirit, to sustain me." I was crying out to God to give me a willing spirit to embrace the season I found myself in. I knew that if I were going to turn the corner and change my mourning into dancing once again, it would be by no other means than God alone restoring joy to my life. I was going to have to learn to praise Him on the mountain and in the valley all the same. He could not just be good when things were going the way I wanted. My circumstances do not dictate God's character. I had to accept that. I had to believe that. He is the same God in the shadows as much as He is in the light.

Could I believe that? Could I really live as if that were true?

In August of 2021, just a few months before the chaos began to ensue in my life, I was in Colorado with the seniors from our school on a retreat. We had hiked a short distance away from the cabins and lodge to a valley in the mountains, surrounded by the beautiful terrain of the Rocky Mountains. While in that spot, we had a devotional and a time of worship. Some of the seniors led worship, and one of the songs they sang was "Highlands." I had never heard that song before that day, but that would be a song the Lord would continue to use to minister to me time and time again in the following year.

One of those same students was a part of our team in Vancouver in January 2022. She sang that song during a worship time one night in our hotel as a team. Tears just began pouring down my face while we sang that song. I knew I was entering a place where I would have to decide whether I could praise God just as much in a season of struggle as I could in a season of success. I was scared because I was not sure if I could. I was terrified of what was ahead, but as I mentioned earlier, throughout that week, God worked in many miraculous ways to remind me that He sees me, He hears me, and He loves me.

I walked into 2022 knowing I would have to praise Him through both some peaks and some valleys. Two years later, I walked out of 2023 knowing that it is entirely possible to do so if we turn to God. With my

TWELVE

strength, it is not possible. But He gives us the ability to praise Him in the peaks and the valleys because He is the one who has overcome the world, and He is in us. We may not be able to do it on our own, but we can do it with Him. Take a moment to pause and listen to the words of "Highlands" by The Worship Initiative.

I pray wherever you find yourself today that you find hope in these truths of the unchanging character of God.

- *You may feel overcome by fear or feel completely alone, but you can rest in the One who is faithful to keep His promises.*
- *Even though you may feel as if you are being slain, God is on your side, and He is all you need.*
- *The goodness of God is all around you and running hard after you.*
- *God is a firm foundation on which you can stand; you are safe with Him.*
- *As hard as it may be to quiet the noise surrounding you, listen for the Lord and look for Him. God is at work.*
- *God has taken your brokenness and made it beautiful. He redeems our lives and our story.*
- *Rather than looking upon you with shame, God looks upon you with perfect love.*
- *God is just as good today as He was when He first made Himself known to you.*
- *You can praise the Lord in all circumstances. He is just as near in the light as He is in the darkness.*

God sees you. God hears you. God loves you.

Chapter 10

"Evermore"

John 15:11 says, "I have told you this so that my joy may be in you and that your joy may be complete."

Every year, one of the "Questions of the Day" in my class was: "Mountains or beach?" That is a simple question, but it can lead to a significant build-up of controversy. But the correct answer is mountains every single time.

Yellowstone National Park was my final stop during my time away. Yellowstone National Park was the first National Park and contains many of the infamous sites we have all grown up hearing about, with its multitude of hot springs and geysers. However, what does not receive the hype that it should is the Grand Canyon of Yellowstone.

For my last full day in the parks before beginning my descent South, I decided to get up early and head to the Grand Canyon of Yellowstone to watch the sunrise. I ended up spending about two hours

TWELVE

there that morning just admiring the power and might of God's creation. The colors within the rock walls of the canyon were astounding. The beautiful yellow and orange in the sunrise over the canyon were inspiring. I found myself almost paralyzed from admiration of our incredible Creator. His artistry is beyond comprehension.

The rest of the day, I had planned to go to a coffee shop and spend time processing through what all the days before had held for me. I was going to sit and be with Jesus, reflecting on what had transpired in the nine days leading up to that point, and embrace my final moments in the National Parks. Everything you just read up to this point is what I spent that day processing. The Lord had already been working through all of that with me, but that day, he tied it all up with a ribbon and put a beautiful bow on top as the grand finale.

As I sat at the coffee shop, savoring my delectable chai latte, I finally found the words to express what I knew to be true all along. But this time I could say it and believe it. God was, is, and will always be with me. God's promise to us is His presence. God's plan for us is that we would welcome His presence. God's purpose for us is to enjoy His presence. These are just some of the many passages of scripture that speak to the delightful gift He has given us: His presence.

- Deuteronomy 31:6 says, "Be strong and courageous. Do not be afraid or terrified because of them, for the Lord your God goes with you; he will never leave you nor forsake you."
- Psalm 16:11 says, "You make known to me the path of life; you will fill me with joy in your presence, with eternal pleasures at your right hand."

"EVERMORE"

- Psalm 23:4 says, "Even though I walk through the darkest valley, I will fear no evil, for you are with me; your rod and your staff, they comfort me."
- Psalm 139:7-10 says, "Where can I go from your Spirit? Where can I flee from your presence? If I go up to the heavens, you are there; if I make my bed in the depths, you are there. If I rise on the wings of the dawn, if I settle on the far side of the sea, even there your hand will guide me, your right hand will hold me fast."
- Isaiah 43:2 says, "When you pass through the waters, I will be with you; and when you pass through the rivers, they will not sweep over you. When you walk through the fire, you will not be burned; the flames will not set you ablaze."
- John 15:11 says, "I have told you this so that my joy may be in you and that your joy may be complete."

I sat there at that coffee shop with the biggest smile on my face, rejoicing in God reminding me that His presence is all that I have ever needed. That smile very quickly turned to tears of joy streaming down my face in gratitude that it did not matter if I was in Oklahoma, Wyoming, or Montana, it did not matter if I was single, married, or divorced, it did not matter if I was eight years old, nineteen years old, or thirty-four years old, God's presence was readily available to me. He was not going anywhere. He had never gone anywhere. He had been with me through all of it.

God's promise, plan, and purpose for me that day were the same as they had always been: to know Him deeply and to make Him known. The greatest gift He could ever give me is Himself, and He has offered Himself to me fully.

TWELVE

In those moments of constantly battling the struggle of perfectionism, I had to come to realize that His love could neither be bought nor earned. It was a gift. It was a gift that He gladly and graciously offered in His kindness to me if I would receive it.

In those moments of feeling too much and not enough all at the same time, I had to come to realize that the God of all creation can handle anything I am feeling or experiencing because He has endured it all Himself. Nothing is too big for Him. He is the only One who can truly carry the weight of the world.

In those moments when I felt like I needed to keep my head low and hide away because life did not go the way I thought it should, I had to come to realize that God can use anything we lay at His feet for His glory. This very moment was no exception.

Everything changes when we lock our eyes on Him. The problems of the world dim in comparison to the light of life that we find in Him. What I came to grasp that day entirely was that His presence was not a promise just to provide comfort. God's presence is a promise intended to have a lasting impact on how we live our lives. There is a purpose in His presence. His purpose is that we would enjoy Him.

As we grow increasingly present with God and live in His presence, something within us changes. Suddenly, we desire what God desires. Our heart loves the way His heart loves. I want to take that purpose further. God's purpose for us is to enjoy His presence, most certainly, but that is not all. Enjoying His presence in turn leads us to desire that others also enjoy His presence. Think back to the blind man Jesus healed. He had experienced Jesus' presence. He could not contain himself from

"EVERMORE"

proclaiming to everyone around him the magnificence of encountering God Himself.

On my last day in Yellowstone National Park, I finally reached that place. I had spent a year trying to hide under the radar. I had spent a year allowing the enemy to convince me that I needed to withdraw and hold myself back from being a vessel of truth for the Lord. I let him persuade me that I needed to stay quiet, remain in my lane, and keep to myself.

That had never been me before as an adult. I am deeply relational. I am passionate about the gospel. I am someone who deeply desires for all people to know the love of the Lord. I zealously proclaim God's faithfulness, which I have seen throughout my life, to just about anyone who will listen. I unashamedly point people to Jesus. I unapologetically pursue the Lord with passion, bringing others alongside me in that pursuit.

It finally dawned on me that the worst possible thing I could do is choose to shut down. Why? Because not only was I neglecting God's presence in my life, but I was also robbing myself of the purpose for which He created me. Something truly changed in me that day. I am cautious about what I share and how I share it about that particular season because I do not feel that the world needs to know the intimate details of our lives. However, I eventually came to see that God could use my willingness to be bold in proclaiming His goodness through it.

He had been showing me glimpses of that all along, that I was hesitant to embrace. Over the last few years, the Lord has provided me with several friendships, both new and old, with women who were walking the same journey. He was giving me community in the most unexpected ways. He was providing people to speak life into me, as well as people I

TWELVE

could speak life into. He was showing me that He could use *even* this for His glory.

> Hebrews 10:19-25 says:
>
> Therefore, brothers and sisters, since we have confidence to enter the Most Holy Place by the blood of Jesus, by a new and living way opened for us through the curtain, that is, his body, and since we have a great priest over the house of God, let us draw near to God with a sincere heart and with the full assurance that faith brings, having our hearts sprinkled to cleanse us from a guilty conscience and having our bodies washed with pure water. Let us hold unswervingly to the hope we profess, for he who promised is faithful. And let us consider how we may spur one another on toward love and good deeds, not giving up meeting together, as some are in the habit of doing, but encouraging one another—and all the more as you see the Day approaching.

To understand the magnitude of what this passage is proclaiming, we have to have an understanding of the Old Testament.

In the Old Testament, a barrier existed between God and His people. The intricate details of the Tabernacle were laid out in Exodus once God rescued Israel from Egypt. In Exodus 26:31-33, it says:

> Make a curtain of blue, purple and scarlet yarn and finely twisted linen, with cherubim woven into it by a skilled worker. Hang it with gold hooks on four posts of acacia wood overlaid with gold and standing on four silver bases. Hang the curtain from the clasps and place the ark of the covenant law behind the curtain. The curtain will separate the Holy Place from the Most Holy Place.

"EVERMORE"

God put the curtain into place for protection. God had made it very clear to the Israelites that He was holy and set apart from them. He was not under their authority. He was not like them. They could not demand anything of Him. Out of protection for them, He separated them from His presence.

The high priest was the one and only Israelite who was permitted to enter God's presence in the Most Holy Place. God gave the high priest specific instructions to follow once per year to enter the Most Holy Place. His purpose in entering was to make a sacrifice to atone for the sins of the Israelites. It was a gift to enter the Most Holy Place, which the high priest would have recognized was rooted entirely in God and not himself, because, remember, he was entering to atone for his sin as well as the sins of the rest of Israel. He would have been fully aware that he did not deserve to be in God's presence. He did not deserve the honor of being the high priest. All of it was rooted in who God was (and still is today).

Hebrews 1-9 makes it abundantly clear that because Jesus was the perfect, spotless Lamb, He was the final substitute for sin. He was the final sin offering. He was the final payment needed. He made a way for humanity to no longer be separated from God. We are no longer dependent on a high priest to enter God's presence on our behalf once a year because Christ has already been sacrificed. He is our substitutionary atonement. What does substitutionary atonement mean?

Second Corinthians 5:21 says, "God made him who had no sin to be sin for us, so that in him we might become the righteousness of God." First Peter 2:24 says, "'He himself bore our sins' in his body on the cross, so that we might die to sins and live for righteousness; 'by his wounds you

TWELVE

have been healed.'" We could never have healed ourselves. We could never cleanse ourselves. Jesus took it upon himself to do so. Through His sacrifice, He not only made a way to forgive us of our sins, but He also made a way for us to experience God's presence.

Matthew 27:50-51 says, "And when Jesus had cried out again in a loud voice, he gave up his spirit. At that moment, the curtain of the temple tore from top to bottom." The veil was and will forever be torn. There is no longer a barrier between God and His people because Jesus fulfilled the need for a sacrifice; He paid the ultimate price for sin (Hebrews 9:22). His sacrifice accomplished so much more than just payment for sin, although it also served that purpose.

Then we come to Hebrews 10:19, where the author says we can enter the Most Holy Place with confidence because of the blood of Jesus. Do not miss the beautiful gift that is our ability to know personally the God who is the Creator and Sustainer of the world, the Alpha and the Omega, the Author and Perfecter of our faith. We get to draw near to Him! Hebrews 10:22 says, "Let us draw near to God with a sincere heart and with the full assurance that faith brings, having our hearts sprinkled to cleanse us from a guilty conscience and having our bodies washed with pure water." The result of confidently entering His presence is sincerity and assurance. What a beautiful gift to receive in return for just being with God. We draw near to Him and He shows us genuine, true love and an unfailing promise of faithfulness. That is quite the exchange right there!

When you realize the transaction taking place in this passage, then verse twenty-three seems like a no-brainer. Hebrews 10:23 says, "Let us hold unswervingly to the hope we profess, for he who promised is faithful."

"EVERMORE"

Our hope resides in Christ alone. He accomplished all that we will ever need on the cross. If we had to rely on ourselves, we would be lost. Our hope resides in the One who always has been and always will be faithful.

Then we arrive at two significant verses for us today, Hebrews 10:24-25, "And let us consider how we may spur one another on toward love and good deeds, not giving up meeting together, as some are in the habit of doing, but encouraging one another—and all the more as you see the Day approaching."

I have lived in the "Bible Belt" my entire life. There are churches on just about every corner. A friend of mine once said, "In Oklahoma, you can kick a rock and hit a Christian." There are multiple churches of well over a thousand members, all within just a few miles of each other here. I want to be delicate but honest in what these two verses are communicating to us even today.

Hebrews 10:24 says, "And let us consider how *we* may spur one another on toward love and good deeds." I want to ensure we understand the heart of this passage. The author of Hebrews makes it clear that the church is essential, but not in the way we often treat it as necessary. We usually view the church as a service to us. We determine where we will attend church based on how we feel it nourishes us and our families spiritually.

- Do I like the worship?
- Do I learn anything from the pastor?
- Does the church have a good children's program, student program, etc.?
- Does the church have a small group I like?

TWELVE

Now hear me. There is a place for ensuring that the church you are investing yourself in is a gospel-centered, biblical church. There is wisdom and discernment that we should be exercising on an ongoing basis in the church we attend, including every single sermon we hear and every song we sing in worship. I am not neglecting that. But do you notice a difference in Hebrews 10:24 and those questions? Hebrews 10:24 paints a picture of the church as a place where we pour out just as much as we are being poured into. Collectively, as the body of Christ, we come together to encourage one another. There is an intentional effort that should be taking place on each of our behalf to be a contributor to the body of Christ, not just to be a consumer.

In other words, our faith is not just personal, though it is that. Our faith is communal. We are dependent on one another. God commands us to prioritize gathering together. It is not always easy or convenient to come together, especially as we draw closer to Christ's return. The anticipation of His coming should compel us to congregate. Yet here I am in an area of the world where many sit as observers every Sunday morning. Or, even worse, you will hear people say they love Jesus, but they hate the church, so no one should expect them to be a part of the church.

Again, please hear my tender heart in responding to this. I understand deeply the wounds that can come as a result of church hurt. I have watched it happen many times over the years, and I have been the recipient of it more than once. The church is full of sinful people. You likely will get hurt by someone, and you also likely will hurt someone over time in the church. This is where wisdom and discernment are critical in the church you choose to immerse yourself in. The expectation should never be that everyone handles everything perfectly in the church. The expectation should be for everyone to strive to respond to everything in a God-honoring way in the church, and when they fail, for them to respond to that failure in a God-honoring way as well. So, when you are the one who hurts someone else, are you willing to seek out that person and take responsibility for the hurt you have caused? If you are not, why would you expect anyone else to do so?

    A healthy church is one where the expectation within the church is for followers of Christ to genuinely encourage one another towards "love and good deeds" which embodies humility, selflessness, and service. In my experience, this is most evident in moments where the heartbeat of the church is to regularly practice confession of sins to one another and pursue reconciled relationships through that confession. When we remind ourselves of our own need for Christ daily, how much more are we filled with His joy? How much more are we filled with His peace? How much more are we filled with His love?

    Many years ago, a friend of mine and I would get lunch every other week and talk through two questions:

How have you been feeding your soul?

How have you been feeding your flesh?

I have no idea where we heard that at the time, but I have heard many pastors and teachers reference similar variations to those two questions over the years. Those same two questions remain, to this day, two of my favorite topics to discuss with friends and with students. Those two questions remind us of two things: 1) We are desperately dependent on God every day of our lives. If we think we can survive on our own, we are

TWELVE

misinformed. 2) We are responsible for what we ingest. Every single thing we put into our bodies (figuratively and literally) has an impact.

We desperately need Christ, but we also desperately need the body of Christ. The body of Christ needs us. Life here on this side of eternity will never be easy. In fact, according to Scripture, we should expect it to get increasingly more difficult. But the Lord works in and through us to help the body of Christ continue to pursue a relationship with Him in this laborious world. John 15:9-11 says:

> As the Father has loved me, so have I loved you. Now remain in my love. If you keep my commands, you will remain in my love, just as I have kept my Father's commands and remain in his love. I have told you this so that my joy may be in you and that your joy may be complete.

The breakthrough for me that day occurred in recognizing that not only was God's presence all that I needed, but He had already offered it to me in His fullness through His love. He was all that I wanted and needed, but He was also with me all along. He was not going anywhere. Throughout my life, I have been able to know Him, see Him, feel Him, and enjoy His presence through my time with Him and my time with other believers. I most certainly have Him with me forever and always. That is never going to change. But I also have the gift of His people in all circumstances. I pray you know the joy that God can fill you with, which can only come from the gift of knowing His presence. I pray that joy would be complete just as His love for you is complete.

Every year, one of my dear friends and I take a weekend to participate in If:Gathering, a women's conference. At If:Gathering 2023, I

"EVERMORE"

heard "Evermore" for the first time. I loved the message of the song from the very first time I heard it, but that day in Yellowstone National Park, that song began to strike a whole different chord in my heart. I am not even exaggerating when I say that I played it no less than five times in a row on one of my drives. I pray the words of this song bless you as well. Take a moment to pause and listen to the words of "Evermore" by Christy Nockels.

I pray wherever you find yourself today that you find hope in these truths of the unchanging character of God.

- *You may feel overcome by fear or feel completely alone, but you can rest in the One who is faithful to keep His promises.*
- *Even though you may feel as if you are being slain, God is on your side, and He is all you need.*
- *The goodness of God is all around you and running hard after you.*
- *God is a firm foundation on which you can stand; you are safe with Him.*
- *As hard as it may be to quiet the noise surrounding you, listen for the Lord and look for Him. God is at work.*
- *God has taken your brokenness and made it beautiful. He redeems our lives and our story.*
- *Rather than looking upon you with shame, God looks upon you with perfect love.*
- *God is just as good today as He was when He first made Himself known to you.*
- *You can praise the Lord in all circumstances. He is just as near in the light as He is in the darkness.*

TWELVE

- *God's presence is His promise, His plan, and His purpose for you. God is with you evermore.*

God sees you. God hears you. God loves you.

Chapter 11

"Falling in Love"

1 John 4:19 says, "We love because he first loved us."

I love Jesus. Like, I *really* love Jesus. I have never been in a context where I felt the need to hide that, regardless of whether I found myself in a faith-based setting or not. To my core, it is my greatest love.

As you are now fully aware, my love for the Lord is not because I ever felt like I deserved His love; it is, in fact, the opposite. I have passionately loved Jesus since I was eight years old because I could see clearly that He first loved me. I could see that He loved me completely. I could see that He loved me unconditionally.

Where I struggled most of my life was with the question of whether God liked me. That may seem so silly, but there is a drastic difference between love and like. But did you know that God likes you? Did you know that He *really* likes you? He *delights* in you.

TWELVE

- Psalm 147:11 says, "The Lord delights in those who fear him, who put their hope in his unfailing love."
- Psalm 149:4 says, "For the Lord takes delight in his people; he crowns the humble with victory."
- Zephaniah 3:17 says, "The Lord your God is with you, the Mighty Warrior who saves. He will take great delight in you; in his love, he will no longer rebuke you, but will rejoice over you with singing."

I adore my son. I love him with every ounce of my being. I delight in him. He brings so much laughter to my life. He brings a lot of adventure to my days. He brings so much warmth to my soul. I genuinely enjoy spending time with him. It does not matter if that time is spent with us jamming out to any of the three High School Musical soundtracks (which we do regularly), attempting to play all of the sports that he is far better at already than I ever have been, or just snuggling up on the floor watching a show or a movie (because for some reason we prefer to make pallets on the floor for things like that than sit on the perfectly good couch we are leaned up against). I love him and I like him.

But did you know God feels the same way about us? He loves us and He likes us. What does that even mean?

Delight brings so much more depth to a relationship than just awareness. I may know someone and even know them well, but to delight in them shows a personal enjoyment of them. It portrays a deep value in them. God loves us as much as He loves Jesus. Just as we love Him for no other reason than because He loved us first, we delight in Him for no other reason than because He delighted in us first. I delight in my time with my son because it is personal to us. We genuinely enjoy being in each other's

"FALLING IN LOVE"

presence. One of the greatest prayers of my heart is that we never stop enjoying quality time together.

In the same way, God genuinely enjoys being in our presence because He knows that as we are in His presence, He transforms us. He becomes our treasure. He becomes our portion. Psalm 73:25-26 says, "Whom have I in heaven but you? And earth has nothing I desire besides you. My flesh and my heart may fail, but God is the strength of my heart and my portion forever."

I told you we were going to come back to Romans 8, and now is that time. Before we keep going, please pause and read over that chapter at least once, if not two or three or four times. Please notice from the very beginning that this chapter makes it clear that the promises that are to follow are "for those who are in Christ Jesus" (Romans 8:1). What does it mean to be in Christ Jesus? Romans 10:9-11 says:

> If you declare with your mouth, "Jesus is Lord," and believe in your heart that God raised him from the dead, you will be saved. For it is with your heart that you believe and are justified, and it is with your mouth that you profess your faith and are saved. As Scripture says, "Anyone who believes in him will never be put to shame."

To be in Christ Jesus means that you recognize that you have sin in your life that you cannot pay the price for yourself, but you believe that Jesus paid that price for you. You confess that sin to the Lord with a desire to turn away from that sin and turn to Him and profess that you recognize that is only possible through Jesus. In return, a beautiful exchange takes place.

TWELVE

Here are ten of the many, many promises we see in this passage of Scripture that come as a result of that exchange:

1. There is no condemnation (v. 1)
2. We have freedom from the law of sin and death (v. 2)
3. The Spirit lives in us (v. 11)
4. We are the children of God (v. 14)
5. The Spirit testifies on our behalf (v. 16)
6. We are heirs of God and co-heirs with Christ (v. 17)
7. The Spirit helps us in our weakness (v. 26)
8. The Spirit intercedes on our behalf (v. 27)
9. God can work all things for good (v. 28)
10. Absolutely nothing can separate us from the love of God (v. 38-39)

Again, those are just a portion of the promises in these passages, but every single promise lays out clearly that it applies only to those who are in Christ Jesus. They are true of every single person who is in Christ Jesus.

Do you see the unfathomable exchange that follows when we lay down our brokenness? Why on earth would God give us all of those promises (and so very many more throughout Scripture) in exchange for us laying down our sinful lives at His feet? There is nothing God loves more than sharing His love with His creation. He delights in all He has made! He wants us to enjoy His presence. He wants us to know His presence. Romans 8:31 says, "What, then, shall we say in response to these things? If God is for us, who can be against us?"

My love for my sweet son grows stronger with each passing day. I thought I loved him fully the day he was born. I most certainly loved him to the fullest extent I was capable of loving him that day. But God has

"FALLING IN LOVE"

shown me throughout motherhood that love is something that continues to grow in us, even in relationships that were rooted in love from the very beginning. Second Thessalonians 1:3 says, "We ought always to thank God for you, brothers and sisters, and rightly so, because your faith is growing more and more, and the love all of you have for one another is increasing."

For anything to grow, it has to be tended to and nurtured. The greatest gift I received as a result of my time away in the mountains was that I went with the full intention of cultivating my relationship with the Lord. The views, scenery, and friendships formed were a bonus. But the time spent allowing the Lord into the depths of my heart was invaluable.

One thing I took away was that I need to make that a regular practice in my life. God fueled the fire within my soul because I allowed Him to pour gasoline on it. I had been letting the worries of the world try to smother it out. I was allowing distractions to shovel dirt in the masses onto a fire that had burned so brightly in my life for so long. But when I opened my hands in complete and total surrender to the Lord, I found myself feeling more seen and loved than I ever had before. Hebrews 12:1-3 says:

> Therefore, since we are surrounded by such a great cloud of witnesses, let us throw off everything that hinders and the sin that so easily entangles. And let us run with perseverance the race marked out for us, fixing our eyes on Jesus, the pioneer and perfecter of faith. For the joy set before him he endured the cross, scorning its shame, and sat down at the right hand of the throne of God. Consider him who endured such opposition from sinners, so that you will not grow weary and lose heart.

TWELVE

Until the fall of 2021, I was not a regular runner. In college, a friend and I would occasionally run the trail that circled our campus, but we would typically run no more than two miles. Then, for some reason, I signed up to run the half-marathon scheduled for April 2022. At that point, the most I had ever run was three, maybe four miles. But even at that point in my life, the idea of Hebrews 12:1 made perfect sense to me.

Who in their right mind wants to run with additional weight on them?

When I ran the half-marathon, some people ran in full firefighter garb right along with me. I did well to run that distance on its own. I cannot even imagine what it would have been like to run that distance with an additional forty-five pounds. The people who chose to do that did not decide that just sounded like a really fun idea. The Oklahoma City Memorial Marathon is in honor of the bombing that took place in our state in 1995. Many choose to run in the firefighter garb as a way to honor those who were the first responders in that particular event. They are making a conscious choice to bear that additional weight because of the weight those men and women bore for our community at that time.

In the race of life, we do not have to carry that extra weight. Jesus took that weight for us. We get to throw it off and run in the freedom that comes from the salvation we receive in Christ. But even without the extra weight, we still have to run the distance. The author of Hebrews also makes it clear that keeping our eyes on Jesus is the only way to have the strength to persevere. He will see us through to the end. Even if at the end of our life we feel like we have been beaten so badly we are like Strip "The King" Weathers on *Cars* being pushed across the finish line by Lightning McQueen, Jesus will get us across that finish line. First Peter 5:6-10 says:

"FALLING IN LOVE"

Humble yourselves, therefore, under God's mighty hand, that he may lift you up in due time. Cast all your anxiety on him because he cares for you. Be alert and of sober mind. Your enemy the devil prowls around like a roaring lion looking for someone to devour. Resist him, standing firm in the faith, because you know that the family of believers throughout the world is undergoing the same kind of sufferings. And the God of all grace, who called you to his eternal glory in Christ, after you have suffered a little while, will himself restore you and make you strong, firm and steadfast.

God loves you fiercely. God calls us to stand firm in our faith, but as we have seen time and time again in Scripture, that comes back to knowing God and His great love. In moments of suffering, it often feels as though God is somehow absent or hiding. But Peter reminded the followers of Christ in the early church, just as He reminds us today, that no matter how hard life may seem right here and right now on this earth, there is a day coming when God will raise us and fully restore us. There is a day coming when God will bring everything to completion. But even in the waiting, He is with us. He loves us. Because He first loved us, we can love Him in return.

My absolute favorite moments in the mountains are not just during the daytime, when looking out over the mountains, hills, and valleys. One of my favorite things to do in life is look at stars, but it is especially wonderful to stargaze in the mountains. When I was growing up, I would often sleep outside on the trampoline in the summer because I found so much comfort in gazing at the stars. Something about seeing the vastness of the universe made the fact that God knew my name and the

TWELVE

hairs on my head somehow even more astounding. Actually, for a brief stint in my childhood, I wanted to be an astronaut. I went to space camp and everything, but that is a story for another time.

But that wonder and amazement I had as a child surveying the stars has not diminished with age. I told you already in college that I drove out to a nearby lake to write in my journal. I always did that at night. The primary reason was that I just wanted to get out of the city and be under the stars. Stargazing in the mountains is next level. When there are no city lights for miles and miles, there is a whole new level of ability to see beyond just the closest of stars. It is nothing short of mesmerizing.

On my last night in Yellowstone National Park, I was determined to sit out and gaze at the stars one last time. But about the time it started getting dark, a storm rolled in. To say I was disappointed is an understatement. But about as quickly as I became disappointed was how quickly that storm moved out. Rainstorms in the summer in the mountains come and go rather quickly.

As I looked up at the stars that night, completely overtaken by God's love, I reiterated Psalm 8:3-4 to myself, "When I consider your heavens, the work of your fingers, the moon and the stars, which you have set in place, what is mankind that you are mindful of them, human beings that you care for them?"

For a reason I will never fully understand, God saw me as an eight-year-old little girl living in Roland, Oklahoma, feeling lost and invisible, and called me His own. He made sure I knew I had been found. He did it all over again when I was fifteen years old, living in Booneville, Arkansas, feeling abandoned and trapped, when He saw me in my pain. He made

"FALLING IN LOVE"

sure I knew He was never going to leave me. He did it all over again when I was nineteen years old, living in Edmond, Oklahoma, feeling unworthy and insignificant, and gave me purpose. He made sure I knew He deliberately made me. He did it all over again when I was thirty-four years old, living once again in Edmond, Oklahoma, feeling afraid and alone, and gave me peace. He made sure I knew that He was with me through it all.

In 2015, we did everything we could have possibly done to move to Vancouver, Canada. If moving countries were as easy as moving states, then Canada is where we would have been living, but alas, it is not. Oklahoma was always a state I thought I would pass through, not my final destination. Our family and friends all knew that once that door opened, we would be moving. When that door would not open, no matter how hard I pushed and pulled, I was initially very disappointed. I did not want to be in Oklahoma.

Then came the last few years of life and all the pain and unrest that came with it. Being in the same place since college meant our community was vast, including relationships from college, our church, and the school where I teach, with overlap in many of those layers as well. Some of those people have been in my life for almost twenty years, while others have been there for just a few years. However, I can tell you without any hesitation that God had us in Oklahoma because He knew that we would need the community we had here in 2022 more than we had ever needed it before. What was just a bonus of where we lived before became essential to survival at that particular time.

Exodus 17:13 says, "When Moses' hands grew tired, they took a stone and put it under him and he sat on it. Aaron and Hur held his hands

TWELVE

up—one on one side, one on the other—so that his hands remained steady till sunset." In this passage, the Israelites were engaged in a war with the Amalekites. When Moses held up his hands with the staff of God, Israel would overpower the Amalekites. But as soon as his hands lowered, they would begin to be overpowered. For Israel to be victorious in the battle, Moses had to remain steadfast. He had to keep his hands in the air. Verse thirteen makes it very clear that Moses was unable to do that on his own. Aaron and Hur had to come alongside him and hold his hands in the air. Because of their help, Moses was able to keep his hands raised, and Israel went on to win the battle. Exodus 17:14 says, "So Joshua overcame the Amalekite army with the sword."

    I can say with absolute certainty that I have stood in a place of battle similar to that of Moses. Had I been standing on my own, the difficult circumstances would have overtaken me. Had I tried to face that fight without the Lord and the community He so graciously provided me, darkness would have prevailed. But God never asked us to fend for ourselves. He tells us quite the opposite in His Word.

- Deuteronomy 3:22 says, "Do not be afraid of them; the Lord your God himself will fight for you."
- Isaiah 41:10 says, "So do not fear, for I am with you; do not be dismayed, for I am your God. I will strengthen you and help you; I will uphold you with my righteous right hand."
- Romans 8:37 says, "No, in all these things we are more than conquerors through him who loved us."

    Through the work of the Lord and the two dear friends who were Aaron and Hur in my life in that season, rather than crumbling in defeat, I

"FALLING IN LOVE"

felt the Lord draw me deeper into the pursuit of Him. There were days I physically, emotionally, and mentally could hardly stand. Two very dear friends never let me think for even a second that I was enduring that season alone. Their ministry of presence to me was exactly what I needed, but the beauty of their hearts was that I also never even had to ask for it. They were just here. They were there via phone calls and texts. They were there in the parking lot wherever I found myself. They were there with a chai latte or a Braum's mix in hand. God worked mightily through them to hold up my weak and weary arms.

Psalm 51:10-12 says, "Create in me a pure heart, O God, and renew a steadfast spirit within me. Do not cast me from your presence or take your Holy Spirit from me. Restore to me the joy of your salvation and grant me a willing spirit, to sustain me." In a time when I could have sat in sackcloth covered in ashes, the Lord instead restored my joy and filled me with a longing for His presence to be known even more personally than it ever had been before. My love for Him grew significantly in that season.

In years past, whenever I went on a trip anywhere, I always felt an internal tension that I had to wrestle with about returning to Oklahoma. But as I drove back to Oklahoma on my final day of the trip, I found myself giddy to be back with my people. Now, let me be clear: watching the temperature gauge in my car go from about 55°F in the morning when I pulled out of my campground at Yellowstone National Park to well over 100°F the evening I arrived back in Oklahoma made me want to turn right on back around. Yet even with the temperature nearly doubling, I found myself in a place of complete gratitude for the people I was driving towards.

TWELVE

That was mainly because the Lord did not just use that difficult season to grow a love for Him, though He most certainly did do that. He used that season to develop an indescribable love for the body of Christ. God used countless people in my life in that season to be an outpouring of His love, empathy, compassion, kindness, gentleness, goodness, and grace. I will be forever grateful for how I saw Him work in and through people of all ages, without them having any idea how badly I was hurting, but simply because they were faithful in responding to the Holy Spirit.

In January 2022, in Vancouver, I shared with a friend the fears that were flooding my mind. We conclude each year's trip with a time of prayer over the students, particularly the seniors. On our last night there, we spent time doing just that. But as soon as we finished, one of the senior girls said she felt like they all needed to stop and pray for me. One by one, each student prayed directly about the exact fears I had expressed to a friend just days before. By the time that prayer ended, I was so overwhelmed by God's sweetness that I was crying, probably the ugliest cry I have ever cried in front of people. I will never forget that moment. God made sure I knew He saw me, He heard me, and He loved me.

In April 2022, a group of students I was beyond blessed to spend countless hours with that year decided that I needed an appreciation week dedicated just to me. Teacher Appreciation Week is typically the first week of May, but they spent the last week of April surprising me with notes and gifts every single day. It all built up to them giving me a necklace in the shape of the country where the precious little boy we had been in the process of adopting was born and currently lived. When they gave it to me, one of the girls said, "We know you are not able to bring him home, but we also know he will forever be a part of your life. We thought this might be a special way to remember him." Once again, there I sat crying an ugly cry. Once again, God made sure I knew He saw me, He heard me, and He loved me.

I also had numerous people reach out to me to tell me the Lord had placed me on their hearts. They would speak encouragement and life directly into the place where I was overwhelmed, without any context of what was transpiring. Truly, God used people of all ages in every area of my life in that season to make sure that in the middle of the storm, I did not miss Him.

You know that feeling in the morning when you wake up and you first turn the light on, how the light is nothing short of blinding? I know the day is coming when my son will be a teenager who grumbles at me for turning the light on to get him out of bed. I very much look forward to that day (said with all the sarcasm in the world). But then, within just a few minutes of the light being on, you do not think anything of it anymore. It is just on. You are used to it. The light is no more or less bright first thing in the morning than it is just ten minutes later. It is our eyes that adjust and change.

I think that the same is true of God's presence in our lives. He is no more or less present in our lives in the peaks than He is in the valleys. His light shines just as bright in the day as it does in the night. However, our awareness of His presence changes drastically based on our surroundings, as our sensitivity to the light shifts in those moments. God's light shines so brightly even in the darkest places, but we have to open our eyes and look for Him. We can either sit there, covering our eyes, waiting for the storm

TWELVE

to pass, hoping it does not overpower us, or we can open our eyes and look for the hand God has graciously extended to us to lead us through the storm.

Psalm 103:11-13 says:

For as high as the heavens are above the earth, so great is his love for those who fear him; as far as the east is from the west, so far has he removed our transgressions from us. As a father has compassion on his children, so the Lord has compassion on those who fear him.

To have compassion on us means God is willing to suffer right along with us. He does not just want to watch us suffer. He is not a bystander in our pain. He does not want us to hurt. He wants to gather us in His arms and heal our broken hearts. He wants to cover us in His comfort and His peace.

Psalm 34:18 says, "The Lord is close to the brokenhearted and saves those who are crushed in spirit." The more I looked for Him in that season, the more I saw Him. The more I saw Him, the more He led me to worship Him. The more I worshiped Him, the more my love just kept growing for Him. Whatever season you find yourself in right now, open your eyes with a willingness to see God working. The more you do, the more your love for Him will grow.

"Falling in Love" has been the outcome of my journey with the Lord in my life, particularly as I have sought to discern where He is at work in the last few years. I pray your love for the Lord only continues to grow as well. Take a moment to pause and listen to the words of "Falling in Love" by Phil Wickham.

"FALLING IN LOVE"

I pray wherever you find yourself today that you find hope in these truths of the unchanging character of God.

- *You may feel overcome by fear or feel completely alone, but you can rest in the One who is faithful to keep His promises.*
- *Even though you may feel as if you are being slain, God is on your side, and He is all you need.*
- *The goodness of God is all around you and running hard after you.*
- *God is a firm foundation on which you can stand; you are safe with Him.*
- *As hard as it may be to quiet the noise surrounding you, listen for the Lord and look for Him. God is at work.*
- *God has taken your brokenness and made it beautiful. He redeems our lives and our story.*
- *Rather than looking upon you with shame, God looks upon you with perfect love.*
- *God is just as good today as He was when He first made Himself known to you.*
- *You can praise the Lord in all circumstances. He is just as near in the light as He is in the darkness.*
- *God's presence is His promise, His plan, and His purpose for you. God is with you evermore.*
- *You can allow yourself to let go and fall deeply in love with the Lord. He is not going anywhere.*

God sees you. God hears you. God loves you.

Chapter 12

"I Will Carry You"

John 16:33 says, "I have told you these things, so that in me you may have peace. In this world you will have trouble. But take heart! I have overcome the world."

We have reached the end already. I am not sure how that happened. I do not know how many hands these words will pass through, but I can assure you it is not because I wanted my name on the cover of a book. I pushed back against this for a few months. The Lord reiterated to me through multiple people that this might be something He would want me to share with others. Each time I just said, "No, no, no, that time with the Lord was for me and Him. I would have to share some of the depths of my heart for all to see, and I am just not sure I can do that."

Then another friend would come along and echo the same thoughts to me, that I should consider writing this down. Just maybe God could use it to bless someone else. I finally decided to entertain the idea

TWELVE

enough to appear obedient to God in this step, which I felt more than unqualified to take.

I finally listened enough to reach out to a friend who had written two books to ask what his process looked like. I was taking what I thought was the most helpful next step of trying to walk in obedience, even in the face of fear and trembling. Still, all the while, I did not know how God could take my jumbled thoughts, prayers, and journals and formulate them into anything as substantial as this.

In some ways, I should not have been surprised, as I am a woman of many words. I have been told more than once by students and friends that I talk more than just about anyone they have ever met. I used Twitter for a very short while. I always hated Twitter because who can convey a message in just 140 characters?! It is no surprise that I came up with around 50,000 words to share the details of this story. However, I can promise you that the ability to write this story and share it has been through the work of God alone.

I very much feel and understand Paul's words in 1 Corinthians 2:1-5 when he says:

> And so it was with me, brothers and sisters. When I came to you, I did not come with eloquence or human wisdom as I proclaimed to you the testimony about God. For I resolved to know nothing while I was with you except Jesus Christ and him crucified. I came to you in weakness with great fear and trembling. My message and my preaching were not with wise and persuasive words, but with a demonstration of the Spirit's power, so that your faith might not rest on human wisdom, but on God's power.

Salvation is only available to us through Jesus. True healing is only available to us through Jesus. Jesus is the only one capable of redeeming us. It is only through Jesus that we can offer anything to anyone in this world that is truly good. John 14:6 says, "Jesus answered, 'I am the way and the truth and the life. No one comes to the Father except through me.'"

We have been offered the means to salvation, healing, and redemption. Although it is a gift freely offered to each of us, it did not come without cost. It came at a price that is far beyond anything we could ever pay on our own. But God in His grace willingly absorbed that cost upon Himself. There is no other response to recognizing the cost of grace on the cross than surrender and love.

As we finish this book, I pray that you will seek hope in Christ alone. I pray that you look to the One who created you to find your worth and your value. I pray that you believe beyond a shadow of a doubt the promises of God that He sees you, He hears you, and He loves you. He will never leave you. He is with you in every single moment of every single day of your life.

Hebrews 13:20-21 says:

> Now may the God of peace, who through the blood of the eternal covenant brought back from the dead our Lord Jesus, that great Shepherd of the sheep, equip you with everything good for doing his will, and may he work in us what is pleasing to him, through Jesus Christ, to whom be glory for ever and ever. Amen.

That is my prayer for you and me. Fix your eyes upon Jesus. Hold tightly to Him. Trust Him, no matter where you may be standing at this moment. He is sure and steady. He will equip you with everything you need. He will lead

TWELVE

you and guide you. Trust that He is holding you tightly. He loves you completely.

Surround yourself with other believers. You need the body of Christ, and the body of Christ needs you. Submerge yourself in that body. It will take effort. It will take time. But that body should be like a family. If your family does not know Jesus, that body will likely become closer than your biological family. Be a part of encouraging others towards love and good deeds, and allow them to do the same for you.

The week after I returned to Oklahoma from my trip, I sat down to re-read and process all the notes I had written from my time away. I wrote this as a summation of what the Lord was reminding me of throughout that season. Here is my heart laid bare for you once again.

"Sought"

I have spent the last year hiding in the shadows

I was too scared to walk out of the shallows

I felt like if I did, I would end up in the gallows

I had no desire to be the cause of tornadoes

I had let the lies consume each and every thought

That I was best left with my stomach in a knot

You found me and reminded me I had been bought

The battle I was facing had already been fought

I could let go, knowing I would always be caught

You found me and told me I had been sought

"I WILL CARRY YOU"

I needed to know I had a place to belong
A child of the King who was loving and strong
Your right hand had been there all along
Giving me shelter, breath, and a new song

I had let the lies consume each and every thought
That I was best left with my stomach in a knot
You found me and reminded me I had been bought
The battle I was facing had already been fought
I could let go, knowing I would always be caught
You found me and told me I had been sought

You take broken people and make them new
The valley of death you led me through
You used that season to draw me after you
I truly depended on you, and my love grew

I had let the lies consume each and every thought
That I was best left with my stomach in a knot
You found me and reminded me I had been bought
The battle I was facing had already been fought
I could let go, knowing I would always be caught
You found me and told me I had been sought

Thank you for showing me you were not done
No matter what comes, to You I want to run

TWELVE

> You've redeemed me by the works of the Son
> There's nothing to fear, You've already won
>
> I had let the lies consume each and every thought
> That I was best left with my stomach in a knot
> You found me and reminded me I had been bought
> The battle I was facing had already been fought
> I could let go, knowing I would always be caught
> You found me and told me I had been sought

Precious friend, I am not an exception to the rule. God does not love me any more than He does you. I can assure you, I am no more deserving of His love than you. I can promise you that the same God who walked with Shadrach, Meshach, and Abednego in the fire in Daniel 3 is the same God who has walked with me through the darkest of days in my life. But more than that, I can promise you that He is the same God walking with you wherever you find yourself today.

In a season when I felt like I could not persevere on my own, God reminded me that I felt that way because it was true. I could not persevere on my own. I was going to have to let Him help me. I was going to have to let the body of Christ help me. However, as I did, I received a great deal of freedom as a result.

I started to see God's love through Him and the body of Christ in that time, vividly. His love was so tender and sweet to me during that season, and it remains so today. There is nothing that you or I can do to make God love either of us any more than He already does. But there is also nothing you or I can do to make God love either of us any less. His love is perfect. His love is complete.

Matthew 11:28-30 says:

Come to me, all you who are weary and burdened, and I will give you rest. Take my yoke upon you and learn from me, for I am gentle and humble in heart, and you will find rest for your souls.

For my yoke is easy and my burden is light.

Do you see where that passage starts? It starts with us coming to Him. We go to Him and He takes the heavy weight we are trying to carry on our own. He removes it from our shoulders and carries it for us. He is gentle. He is humble. He is kind.

I am intimidated by gyms and all of the machines. I would rather run or just have my little dumbbells that I work out with at home. That is more my type of exercise. In my mind, a gym comes with someone screaming at you to keep pushing and keep going, while you try with all of your might to raise that bar with all the added weights above your chest or your head before it just comes right back down. Then you repeat the process again and again. That just sounds like torture.

I do not respond well to yelling. If you want me to shut down quickly, all you need to do is yell at me. I despise it. That is not motivating to me. If a coach were to yell at me, it would not encourage me to try harder. It would have the exact opposite effect. In fact, in any sport I attempted to participate in, it demotivated me if a coach yelled at me rather than helping me try to understand what I did wrong. That may come from my gymnastics background. In gymnastics, my coach would help explain the change in placement of a part of my body that I needed to

TWELVE

strengthen a skill. I could then adapt and adjust my body to get into the correct position to perform the skill correctly. Many other sports can involve coaches who just yell.

That is not the imagery we see in this passage. When we come before the Lord with this heavy weight, we are so desperate to try to push up on our own to prove our strength, but we are struggling even to be able to get up off the ground. In response to our weakness, He does not yell at us and tell us to push harder. Instead, He grabs the weight for us. He tells us we have nothing to prove. He reminds us that there are burdens we cannot carry because they will not make us stronger; they will just injure us. He takes the weight. But He also takes us. He takes us to a place where we can rest. That place is with Him. We find rest with Him. We find rest in His presence.

Psalm 62:1-2 says, "Truly my soul finds rest in God; my salvation comes from him. Truly, he is my rock and my salvation; he is my fortress, I will never be shaken." Do you feel rested? Or do you feel like your feeble knees are about to come crashing to the ground from trying to hold up the weight of life as long as humanly possible on your own?

Sweet friend, set it down. You have nothing to prove. Jesus has already proven to us that He is the only one who can carry that weight. Just let it go. Let Him have it. He's got it. Trust Him enough to lay it at His feet, and know that He will take care of it. He will take care of you. He loves you.

If you find yourself in a place like I did, where it is not just you being affected, know that God has all of you. God will take care of every single one of us as we turn to the Lord. God loves your child even more than you do. God loves your spouse even more than you do. God loves your parents

"I WILL CARRY YOU"

even more than you do. God loves your friend even more than you do. Whomever it is, God loves them. God loves them with a perfect love. Trust Him to love them far better than you ever could.

I know it can be scary to surrender yourself and others into God's hands. But you are surrendering them to the One who has already won. Revelation is such a fascinating book of the Bible, but what is amazing is that the book, as complex and challenging to comprehend as it is, can be boiled down to just a few words: God has *already* won! Do you believe that? Do you believe that whatever battle you find yourself waging in a war against, He has already won?

Sin - He defeated it. Sickness - He defeated it. Death - He defeated it. Sorrow - He defeated it. Shame - He defeated it. Guilt - He defeated it. Fear - He defeated it. He defeated it *all*.

There is a day coming when that defeat will be on full display when He also destroys it. It will be no more. Revelation 21:1-4 says:

> Then I saw "a new heaven and a new earth," for the first heaven and the first earth had passed away, and there was no longer any sea. I saw the Holy City, the new Jerusalem, coming down out of heaven from God, prepared as a bride beautifully dressed for her husband. And I heard a loud voice from the throne saying, "Look! God's dwelling place is now among the people, and he will dwell with them. They will be his people, and God himself will be with them and be their God. 'He will wipe every tear from their eyes. There will be no more death or mourning or crying or pain, for the old order of things has passed away.'"

TWELVE

That day is what we long for! God created us to long for Heaven. Ecclesiastes 3:10-11 says, "I have seen the burden God has laid on the human race. He has made everything beautiful in its time. He has also set eternity in the human heart; yet no one can fathom what God has done from beginning to end."

Did you know that for everything we long for, there is a way to fulfill it? For hunger, there is food. For thirst, there is water. Every longing we have has an ultimate realization. This place we long for, where there will be no more sin, sickness, death, sorrow, shame, guilt, fear, and anything else in this life that we have grown to hate, it is a place that exists. It has an ultimate fulfillment in Heaven. Christ is the only thing that can truly fulfill us.

Romans 3:22 says, "This righteousness is given through faith in Jesus Christ to all who believe. There is no difference between Jew and Gentile." If you have never accepted the gift God has been so graciously extending to you all the days of your life, there is no better time than the present. I can assure you that there is absolutely nothing in your life that is too big, bad, or scary for Him. He can handle it. He can lift the weight. He is the only One who can lift the weight. So, let Him. You have everything to lose if you do not let Him. You have everything to gain if you do let Him.

God has already come to you through His Son. The question is, will you go to Him? Romans 10:10 says, "For it is with your heart that you believe and are justified, and it is with your mouth that you profess your faith and are saved."

From the deepest place of my heart, I want you to know the compassion and love I have for you and the place you find yourself right

"I WILL CARRY YOU"

now. I would love nothing more than to grab a chai latte and sit and hear your stories of God's goodness in your life, even on the hardest day. I pray this story has only reminded you all the more that He truly is good. His goodness is all around us. I am thankful to be standing where I am now and be able to look back and say with certainty that I am where I am today because of God alone working in me and through others to bring me to this very spot.

I am trusting each word of this book into His hands. It is intimidating and unnerving to me to trust it in the hands of anyone else, but in reality, I am not. I am trusting it into His hands. If nothing else, He has used each word to remind me of who He is and who He has always been. That is worth it.

One year, as my friend and I went away for another If:Gathering conference, we tacked on a Drew and Ellie Holcomb concert in our weekend getaway. That weekend happened to be in March of 2022, the week after the metaphorical natural disaster struck my life. Ellie sang "I Will Carry You." I had already listened to that song countless times that week because I felt that song to the deepest part of my being in that given moment. But hearing her sing it in person led to my eyes welling up with tears. I closed my eyes and just let the truth of the song flood my mind. God was not walking away from me. He was going to carry me. The same is true for you. God is not going to walk away from you. He will carry you. Take a moment to pause and listen to the words of "I Will Carry You" by Ellie Holcomb.

I pray wherever you find yourself today that you find hope in these truths of the unchanging character of God.

TWELVE

- You may feel overcome by fear or feel completely alone, but you can rest in the One who is faithful to keep His promises.
- Even though you may feel as if you are being slain, God is on your side, and He is all you need.
- The goodness of God is all around you and running hard after you.
- God is a firm foundation on which you can stand; you are safe with Him.
- As hard as it may be to quiet the noise surrounding you, listen for the Lord and look for Him. God is at work.
- God has taken your brokenness and made it beautiful. He redeems our lives and our story.
- Rather than looking upon you with shame, God looks upon you with perfect love.
- God is just as good today as He was when He first made Himself known to you.
- You can praise the Lord in all circumstances. He is just as near in the light as He is in the darkness.
- God's presence is His promise, His plan, and His purpose for you. God is with you evermore.
- You can allow yourself to let go and fall deeply in love with the Lord. He is not going anywhere.
- God will carry you when you feel like you cannot possibly go on any longer. He will never let you go.

God's Word is a gift given to us to reveal His heart to us. From Genesis to Revelation, we see that He is intentional. He is loving. He is kind. He is patient. He is good.

"I WILL CARRY YOU"

Take heart, sweet friend. God sees you. God hears you. God loves you.

About the Author

Amber Peterson loves Jesus, enjoys deep conversations with a chai latte in hand, and delights in exploring God's beautiful creation. She is the wife of an incredible man of God and the mom of a precious boy, both sweet blessings the Lord uses to sanctify her more each day. Moreover, she is someone who has witnessed the transforming work of the Lord in her life. By Christ alone, she knows that she can come to the throne of grace with confidence, knowing that what He has started in her life He will bring to completion. As long as she has breath, He has a plan and a purpose. She believes with all of her heart that His plan and purpose are for His glory and her good.

Made in the USA
Monee, IL
19 November 2025